Dermot Bolger was born in
The Lament for Arthur C
Beckett Award for best firs
Stewart Parker Award and an ~~Edinburgh~~ ~~~~ ~~~~
High Germany (later filmed by Irish television), **The Holy
Ground** (which also received an Edinburgh Fringe First
Award) and **One Last White Horse**. These four plays were
published by Penguin as **A Dublin Quartet**. He has also
adapted James Joyce's **Ulysses** for the stage (**A Dublin
Bloom**, published by New Island/Nick Hern Books) and
written screenplays for **The Disappearance of Finbar**
(Channel 4) and **Edward No Hands** (RTE/BBC).

He is the author of six novels, including **The Journey Home,
The Woman's Daughter, A Second Life** (all Penguin) and
his latest, **Father's Music**, (Flamingo, 1997). A poet and
publisher, and editor of many anthologies, including **The
Picador Book of Contemporary Irish Fiction**, he lives and
works in Dublin.

In the same series:

Long Black Coat	John Waters (with David Byrne)
A Night in November	Marie Jones
A Dublin Bloom (A free adaptation of *Ulysses*)	Dermot Bolger
The Gay Detective	Gerard Stembridge
This Lime Tree Bower	Conor McPherson
Catalpa	Donal O'Kelly
Greatest Hits: Four Irish One-Act Plays	Antoine Ó Flatharta
	Clare Dowling
	Thomas McLoughlin
	John MacKenna
St Nicholas *The Weir*	Conor McPherson

APRIL BRIGHT
&
BLINDED BY THE LIGHT

Two plays

Dermot Bolger

New Island Books / Dublin
Nick Hern Books / London

April Bright
&
Blinded by the Light
are first published in Ireland in 1997 by
New Island Books
2, Brookside,
Dundrum Road,
Dublin 14
& in Britain by
Nick Hern Books,
14 Larden Road,
London W3 7ST

ISBN 1 874597 59 6 (New Island Books)
1 85459 362 5 (Nick Hern Books)

New Island Books receives financial support from The Arts
Council **(An Chomhairle Ealaíon)**, Dublin, Ireland.

Cover design by Jon Berkeley.
Top cover photo by Amelia Stein of Dawn Bradfield as April and
Eithne Woodcock as Rosie in **April Bright**.
Lower cover photo by Fergus Bourke of
Gerard Byrne as Ollie and Phelim Drew as Pascal in
Blinded by the Light.
Typeset by Graphic Resources.
Printed in Ireland by Colour Books, Ltd.

APRIL BRIGHT

A play in two acts

"Less a haunting than an evocation, Bolger's play explores the ordinary lives of both families — one marked by tragedy and the other by joy — as they struggle to find love and hope in sickness and in health, in birth and in death... *April Bright* is haunted by sorrow. Sometimes love and tenderness and sometimes fear and anxiety gleam beneath, but the memories are always cathartic. In this exploration of sorrow — both imprisoning and liberating — Bolger infuses the pain-wracked lives of two families living in the same house fifty years apart with a deeply effective lyricism, and offers a striking vision of personal reconciliation with the past and the present." — *Sunday Tribune*

"A shining example of theatre, *April Bright* is a thought-provoking and exciting play which should entertain and leave a lasting impression. The interchanging of times and personalities is always imaginative and at times stunning." — *Sunday Express*

"Bolger graphically depicts and condemns the ignorant socio-medical hierarchy of the 1940s, when children as well as adults coughed their way to bloody and painful death in a world that sanctimoniously ignored advances in medicine and perscribed instead incantations to a deaf and merciless god, while handing a leper's bell to every stricken family." — *Sunday Independent*

"A stunning evocation of family life in Dublin just after the war... this is a poignant play with much sadness and grief. But it is also full of hope and love. An excellent night's viewing — don't miss it." — *The Cork Examiner*.

*Author's note on staging — **April Bright***

The action of this play happens simultaneously in the 1940s and the 1990s and — in one scene — in the 1970s. These time frames begin to increasingly intertwine and merge as the play progresses. Lighting and positioning should serve to create separate but simultaneous and interlinking spheres of action on the stage, so that both time frames (or plays within the play) unfold concurrently, with characters from both periods present on stage together, unconsciously haunting each other. In the interest of aiding a clear reading of the text the symbol ••• has been inserted where the focus switches between time periods. This should not however signify a pause or break in the action on stage. The focus should switch between the time-frames as fluidly and cleanly as possible, with the director laying particular emphasis on creating behavioural patterns which allow those characters not engaged in the action at any one moment to be still actively engaged in the world of their own scene, while doing nothing to break the immediate focus on the other scene in progress

Each act occurs in one continuous movement, but there are hinge moments when the action does not stop as such, but when the direction may build in a slight pause for refocusing. Occasionally music may also be used to create changes in mood and atmosphere.

Although the two sets of action are autonomous, the figure of THE CALLER should help to animate and link them through her ability to simultaneously see ANNA and SEAN while also being able to vividly recall in her mind's eye, and give witness to, the memories of those past lives which she is reliving.

Dermot Bolger
Dublin 1997

April Bright was first produced by the Abbey Theatre on its Peacock stage in Dublin, on August 23rd, 1995, before being staged by the Abbey Theatre in Limerick, Cork, Galway, Longford, Dundalk and Kilkenny on its Irish National tour in the autumn of 1995.

Directed by	David Byrne

Cast in order of appearance:

Sean Healy	Denis Conway
Anna Byrne	Sian Quill
April Bright	Dawn Bradfield
Rosie Bright	Eithne Woodcock
The Caller	Fedelma Cullen
Eamon Bright	Eamonn Hunt
Kate Bright	Máire Ní Ghráinne

Designer	Monica Frawley
Lighting Designer	Trevor Dawson
Music	Gerard Grennell
Assistant to Designer	Barbara Bradshaw
Sound	David O'Brien
Stage Director	Micil Ryan
Assistant Stage Manager	Audrey Hession

The play is set in an empty house in Dublin.

The author would like to express his sincere thanks to everyone involved in this first production, especially its director, David Byrne.

In memory of a lost uncle,
Francis Bolger,
b: Wexford, 1911, d: Wexford 1928.

Act One

Scene One

Darkness. There is a steady ticking, as if the house itself is counting time. Lights come up dimly enough for us to discern the outline of the set which consists of a split-level house. The entire front half of the stage serves as a kitchen area, with a battered old table to the far left with some rubbish and two battered chairs on top of it. There are three entrances to this lower area, a real door stage bottom left and hidden openings in the wings stage left (beyond the door) and stage right. The one above the door is used sparingly, as a concealed and ghostly entrance, when the door is open, allowing people to appear from behind the door, as if from nowhere. The offstage area stage right would be understood to lead to the scullery and then out into the back garden and the shed.

Further back up stage walls protrude out slightly from both wings to form an arch which frames the more narrow raked bedroom area occupying the back of the stage, which is dominated by an old brass bed with a bare horsehair mattress. These walls allow for two more hidden entrances (on the stage left and right) from behind which actors can simply appear and disappear in the bedroom, as if ghosts from nowhere. There is a light-cord stage left of the bed and the shape of a window (created by the reflection of light, coming in from the stage left). There is also an actual visible bedroom door on the stage right.

In half-light we hear a front door open, footsteps and then the kitchen door opens. Extra light filters through to show us

SEAN HEALY and ANNA BYRNE, a young couple entering and standing uncertainly, hand and hand, in the kitchen. In his spare hand SEAN carries two plastic refuse sacks, one containing sheets and pillows and the other a duvet. They step forward, peering round in the semi-darkness, shocked by the bare state of the kitchen. Almost without noticing it, they let go each others hand and step slightly apart. ANNA is over seven months pregnant. Although there is nervous tension and friction between them, a great tenderness underlies their relationship as they embark on this adventure.

ANNA: Holy God, it's...

The sentence fades. She cannot continue. A look of desolation crosses SEAN'S face which he tries to hide as he drops the bags beside the door.

SEAN: I didn't think it would look half as bad, Anna. (*He crosses over to flick on the light and take the chairs down from the table*) It's no wonder the bastard of a guard got us drunk every night we came down. With the wife sitting there knitting without a word. (*Whining voice*) "And, of course, there's carpets, curtains and fittings free." (*Ordinary voice*) We should be paid to take them.

ANNA: (*Uncertain, non-committally*) They were good quality in their day, I suppose.

SEAN: Yeah, but the Normans made shite of them bringing in the animals to sleep by the fire.

ANNA: (*Quietly*) Please... don't...

SEAN: What?

ANNA: I don't need constant cheering up.

SEAN: I'm sorry, it's just that this was meant to be... I just wanted everything perfect for you. (*ANNA looks around. We feel how desperately SEAN wants her approval.*) Though I suppose at this time of night anywhere is going to look...

ANNA: (*Distracted*) What's that ticking noise?

SEAN: It was madness coming here this late. (*He crosses the stage to look into the wing*) It's an old-fashioned timer switch. (*Looks back at ANNA*) Maybe we'd better go home again for tonight.

ANNA: This is our home. You decided. (*Sees he is hurt*) Alright, I know, we decided.

SEAN: It just feels so shabby without the furniture.

ANNA: We were happy in that apartment.

SEAN: (*Lacking conviction*) And we'll be happy here too.

ANNA: (*With sudden anxiety*) Will we? Are you sure? I mean, you don't think it will change things, Sean? I've told you I'd sooner never own a house if it meant things were going to be different between us.

SEAN: I'm just a bit rattled, love. Take off your coat.

ANNA fingers the top button, about to undo it, then stops and hugs the coat more tightly to her. She sees SEAN staring at her.

ANNA: (*Looks around*) I've nowhere to hang it. I just want to scrub the whole place first.

SEAN: Ah now, be fair, the Bennetts left the place clean.

SEAN takes his own coat off and briefly exits to leave it and the plastic bags in what would be the hallway.

ANNA: Yeah, but it's somebody else's clean. It's not ours...

SEAN: (*Returning*) Give it time, we'll make it ours. Come on, Anna, This is what we've talked of for years. I thought we'd be celebrating.

She approaches, a little reluctantly and they embrace.

SEAN: These days I'm half afraid to hug you.

ANNA: I'm not that fragile, you know.

SEAN: (*Tenderly*) Fragile isn't the word.

ANNA: (*Shivers*) It's cold in here, or at least it feels cold.

SEAN: (*Kneading her shoulders*) That's tension, I can feel it in your shoulders.

ANNA: I'm just a bit rattled too. I didn't sleep well, all the thoughts of moving... the most childish dreams when I did. Some old witch or something and a ginger tomcat coming in a window. Amazing something that silly could be frightening. You don't suppose Bennett had cats here?

SEAN: That fellow pay for cat food, are you joking?

ANNA: (*Laughing, more relaxed*) You know, I thought they'd never leave.

SEAN: We should have waited until our stuff comes in the morning.

ANNA: You didn't take much persuading... standing across in the bushes in the park.

SEAN: Did you see that old wardrobe they loaded onto the van? Definitely Dracula's coffin.

ANNA shifts and moves away. SEAN regrets his turn of phrase.

ANNA: (*Looking around uneasily*) The place will look better in the morning.

SEAN: You still hold it against me, don't you?

ANNA: No.

SEAN: Anna?

ANNA: (*Refusing to be drawn*) Has the new bed arrived at least?

SEAN: (*Slightly peeved*) You go on up and check. Bennett said he'd leave it upstairs to be assembled.

ANNA goes to exit and then stops.

ANNA: Are you coming?

SEAN: (*Getting his own back slightly*) Afraid on your own?

ANNA: No... yes... silly. Ah shag you then.

ANNA exits into hallway. SEAN follows to the door and makes a mock ghostly noise.

ANNA: (*Offstage, both cross and amused*) Sean!

SEAN looks around, with any bravado stripped away. He exits briefly and returns with a spare plastic sack. He puts it on the table and then exits stage right as ANNA enters the half-lit bedroom timidly, almost expecting somebody to be there. Looking slightly lost, she touches the old bedstead, then crosses to the window, where a light switch cord hangs down, attached to a bare bulb. She flicks the light on for a moment, then flicks it off to stare out.

ANNA: (*To herself*) Just the shapes of sheds and the trees in the college. Remember all those nights cycling home alone. Was there somebody out there for you, would you ever find him? (*She flicks the light on as if gazing at her own reflection*) Now I see you, in the window of your own house. Say it. Try to say it. (*She touches her stomach*) Now I see you, like in a picture. Now I see you... (*She flicks the light off*) now I don't.

She flicks the light back on as SEAN re-enters the kitchen, carrying two more battered wooden chairs. The bare bulb above ANNA flickers out, startling her just as SEAN planks the chairs loudly down beside the table. ANNA quickly flicks the light back on and exits. SEAN has begun to put the rubbish on the table into the refuse sack. ANNA appears in the kitchen doorway and SEAN senses her anxiety which she is annoyed with herself for displaying.

SEAN: Are you okay?

ANNA: (*Pointing to the chairs*) Where did you get those?

SEAN: The shed. Crammed with that junk Bennett swore he'd shift. You could open an antique shop out there. Bennett said it was there when he moved in.

ANNA: I bet they're covered in woodworm,

SEAN: I could probably sand these down...

ANNA: We'll burn every stick of it.

SEAN: (*Teasing*) This couldn't be Miss "No Aluminium Windows" who spent the past year dragging me around antique shops?

ANNA: Things in shops are different... they're not personal.

SEAN stares at the floor, stamps his foot suddenly and points towards the tip of his toe.

SEAN: (*Sternly*) Get back into that chair, yous bastards! Go on, about face, hop to it! (*He looks at ANNA*) Legions of woodworm in full battle-dress, shovels tied to their backs. Alright, Hallowe'en comes early this year. No doubt Bennett had every scrap merchant in Dublin up for a gander before he dumped it on us. Anyway, do you remember that shop off the Coombe?

ANNA: Those chairs with the lovely cushions? (*Thrilled*) You didn't, Sean, did you?

SEAN: No... I couldn't afford to. But I bought two of the packing cases the cushions came in.

ANNA goes to playfully strike him and he catches her hands, pulling her into an embrace.

ANNA: (*Softly*) You bastard. Landing this place on me.

SEAN: You were thrilled to have it all arranged just the same. I look after you.

ANNA holds the moment but refuses to be drawn.

ANNA: Bennett left the old bed that he swore he'd shift from upstairs.

SEAN: The one in the baby's bedroom?

ANNA: (*Quickly*) Don't call it... the baby's.

SEAN: That's where we've agreed to put the child.

ANNA: I just don't like calling it her room. Not yet.

SEAN: The child's going to be fine or they would have kept you in hospital. So don't... not tonight...

ANNA: It was different for you.

SEAN: It was never. Now come on, please. A new house.

ANNA: Bought behind my back.

SEAN: You wanted it too. You said you did. Now you know that some woman put in a bid for it. It would have been sold by the time the doctors let you out.

ANNA: You still could have consulted me before paying the deposit at least.

SEAN: The last thing you needed was more pressure. I just wanted a fresh start to make up for everything, somewhere away from the bad memories.

ANNA: (*Looks round again*) The place just feels so strange with the Bennetts gone.

SEAN: I know. We've been caged up in those apartments for too long.

ANNA: (*Suddenly anxious*) Maybe it was better there, owning nothing. We had it so lovely, and the little balcony... (*Sudden desperation*) Sean, I'm sorry but this looks such a God awful desperate kip!

SEAN: (*Totally rattled himself*) Fuck it! I've made a balls of it as usual. (*He storms offstage left towards the ticking fuse box*) Stupid fucking noise!

ANNA: Sean, you'll electrocute yourself!

We hear banging offstage as SEAN works.

SEAN: (*Offstage*) We've bought the bloody kip, lock, stock and barrel. We can smash it to pieces if we want.

ANNA: Sean, be careful, please! Don't... *He returns with the timer switch in his hand as she runs towards him. He holds the switch up, stopping her.*

SEAN: (*Calmer*) Just killing the noise. Listen to that silence now.

In the stillness there is the sudden creak of a door which startles them both.

SEAN: What the hell is that? Maybe it's next door. I'm going up.

SEAN exits. Left alone, ANNA looks around the kitchen.

ANNA: Sean, you're not leaving me here.

ANNA exits as SEAN cautiously enters the bedroom. He looks around, not noticing ANNA who now enters the bedroom as well.

ANNA: Nothing?

SEAN turns, momentarily startled.

SEAN: It was the woodworm leaving. I told you not to mention a bonfire.

ANNA: (*Laughs with relief*) We never had this much fun moving into the apartment. (*Teasing*) You arriving on your bike.

SEAN: (*Smiles*) Ah, don't start that old story again.

ANNA: I'm leaving home and he's not, I said to myself. Lugging four suitcases over to the apartment and he turns up with a plastic bag on his bike.

SEAN: (*Grins*) It wasn't meant that way...

ANNA: A change of clothes... that's how long he think we're going to last, and me after giving up everything. In the bedroom I was, crying by myself.

SEAN: I'd brought the essential things. Toothbrush...

ANNA: Presuming I'd bring the toothpaste...

SEAN: ...change of socks, red bulb, my action underpants...

ANNA: That awful brown pair. We set fire to them and they didn't so much burn as melted. What the hell were they made of?

SEAN: They served me and my family well... ten happy years...

ANNA: (*Teasing*) Play acting. A plastic bag on a bike.

SEAN: Well, I'm not play acting now. We'll look back and think we never really lived there. Owning a house will be different.

ANNA: (*Gently*) Even a kip like this.

SEAN: This is no kip. It's been neglected, that's all, like time's been allowed stand still. It must have looked beautiful once. We'll make it beautiful again. Just wait till we even get our few bits and pieces in. (*Looks around*) I knew this house was for us the moment I saw it. I was born in one like this. Solid Portland stone.

ANNA: It was the view from this window that brought me back to see it twice, the way the sun must come in here in the morning.

SEAN: (*Softly*) Will we go home or stay?

ANNA: Stay. Make a start. The new bed has arrived at least.

SEAN: The old one could be useful too.

ANNA: I'm not sleeping in this!

SEAN: I wasn't thinking of sleep.

ANNA: You must be joking.

SEAN: (*Teasing*) Floorboards are fierce hard on my knees.

ANNA: (*Teasing back*) Well, you needn't do any sanding till tomorrow so.

SEAN: A bit of French polishing?

SEAN tries to catch her, but ANNA moves to one side. He circles playfully, with ANNA shadowing him so that the bed remains between them. She tries to climb across it and he catches her so they both kneel on the mattress. She stops struggling. They kiss, then part, staring at each other's faces as SEAN slowly undoes the first two buttons of ANNA's blouse. He puts his hand softly inside to rest on her breast.

SEAN: All these years... I still love undressing you.

ANNA: (*With a nervous glance round*) What if the Bennetts?

SEAN: Lock, stock and barrel. It's ours.

ANNA: (*Softly*) Be careful.

They lean forward and kiss for a moment before there is a loud knocking on the door. They jerk apart, startled.

SEAN: Who the hell is that?

ANNA: Bennett must have left something.

SEAN: If he did it's well hidden.

ANNA: It's not for us, whoever it is. Ignore them and they'll go away.

The knocking comes again, even louder.

SEAN: What if it's a neighbour? They've have seen us move in.

ANNA: Leave it, Sean.

SEAN: We can't be rude. You wait here.

SEAN climbs from the bed and exits from the bedroom. ANNA goes to follow, then realises that her blouse is half-open.

ANNA: (*Calling after him*) Sean, wait for me! Can't you see I'm not ready? Sean...

She stops, annoyed that SEAN has abandoned her and a little nervous at being alone. She hurriedly buttons up her blouse, looks around at the room and then exits.

● ● ●

Over music the kitchen door opens and THE CALLER enters almost reluctantly. She is in her sixties and dressed in black. She stops, just inside the door and looks around, uncomfortable and yet taking everything in. She carries a bottle wrapped in a brown paper bag. She walks slowly past the protruding wall, from behind which ROSIE BRIGHT (a teenage girl in a 1940s school uniform) emerges upstage, with her steps exactly mirroring THE CALLER's. THE CALLER turns in the kitchen as SEAN appears in the doorway and ROSIE repeats her movement in the bedroom.

● ● ●

ROSIE: It's Daddy! Daddy's back. He's forgotten his sandwiches.

● ● ●

THE CALLER: (*Hesitantly, about to leave again*) I'm sorry, I shouldn't be bothering you.

SEAN: No, please...

THE CALLER: I should have just left it on the doorstep, I didn't mean to knock.

SEAN: No, you're our first visitor.

ANNA *appears briefly, unnoticed, in the kitchen doorway, looks at* THE CALLER *and then exits again.*

THE CALLER: (*Holding the bottle out to SEAN*) Really, all I wanted was to give you this.

SEAN: I'm sorry it's so cold. We haven't actually moved in yet. (*He glances behind, uncertain if ANNA has been there*) Anna? (*To THE CALLER*) I'll just get my... (*He turns and exits, calling*) Anna, it's a neighbour!

● ● ●

THE CALLER turns to look at KATE, a middle-aged woman, who appears in the kitchen from stage right, with an apron over her 1940s-style dress and carrying a sweeping brush. She is smoking and continues to chain-smoke throughout the entire play.

KATE: (*Calling*) April Bright! Your father's lunch is on the table.

APRIL: (*Calling, offstage*) What would that man forget?

KATE: He'd forget his head.

KATE crosses to exit stage left, calling.

KATE: Rosie, there's no use pretending you've a cough like your sister. Get down these stairs and away to school.

THE CALLER has followed KATE's exit with her eyes and now begins to look around at the kitchen. ROSIE starts pacing back and forth in the bedroom, reading from the green covered Catechism notes in her hand. ROSIE stops beside the bed, holds the book to her chest, closes her eyes and tries to recite from memory.

ROSIE: We should alleviate the suffering of the holy souls in Purgatory because... (*She uses her fingers to count*) Our Lord wishes us to; the holy souls suffer much, our own loved ones among them perhaps; they cannot relieve themselves and by us doing so we receive special graces ourselves.

APRIL BRIGHT (a teenage girl in a 1940s dress) enters the bedroom on tiptoes, carrying a quilt. She climbs onto the bed behind ROSIE and puts the quilt over her head like a ghost.

ROSIE: We can alleviate the suffering of the holy souls in Purgatory... (*She uses her fingers again*) by the Holy Mass; by the stations of the cross; by the Rosary; by small acts of penance or self-denial; by... by... blast! (*She opens her eyes and looks at the book in disgust*) by blasted Indulgences. (*Looks up contritely*) Sorry, Lord.

She is making sign of the cross when APRIL makes a ghostly noise, causing ROSIE to turn in fright. APRIL, laughing, falls on top of ROSIE as they both tumble onto the bed.

APRIL: (*Sitting up excitedly*) A corpse, Rosie. Come on quickly, we'll see a corpse.

ROSIE: Where?

APRIL: The top of the road. Old Pointy Nose. Her father's dead. Would you come on. We'll pay our respects.

ROSIE: You mean the old lad who used to sit out on the step in the good weather?

APRIL: Whenever old Pointy Nose let him. Sure the man could barely breathe. Remember the time he called us over to get him ten Sweet Afton in the shop...

ROSIE: I'd almost forgotten him.

APRIL: (*Imitating a rasping whisper*) "Fen Tweet Thfton"... (*Ordinary voice*) and Pointy Nose out like a light in case he gave us any of the change.

ROSIE: I thought he went into some old hospital.

APRIL: Old Pointy Nose had him tucked away in the back bedroom in case he met a young nurse and changed his will. I bet she put a pillow over his head while he slept.

She throws the quilt over ROSIE's head again.

ROSIE: (*Shocked, pulling the quilt off*) God forgive you, April Bright.

APRIL: (*Kneeling to look under bed*) Help me find that set of beads.

The girls kneel, searching under the bed as ANNA enters the bedroom. She crosses to the window, oblivious to their presence, and stares at herself again in the lit window. ROSIE and APRIL rise.

APRIL: Where the hell are those beads?

ROSIE: But sure we can't just go up, we barely even knew him.

APRIL: Ah, will you go away out of that. Theresa and Betty Doran are waiting down at the gate. Sure there'll be such a crowd at the house who's going to be asking questions? (*Thrilled at the thought*) We'll be able to see all the bedrooms in Pointy Nose's house and she won't be able to say a word. I bet you there'll be an Oxford Lunch and probably chocolates. (*Almost hopping with excitement*) Now, will you come on?

ROSIE: (*Looking down at her book*) I've to learn the holy souls in Purgatory.

APRIL: Ah, the nuns. In another six months you'll be rid of them.

ROSIE: I have to learn the holy souls.

APRIL: Listen, Piggy, his holy soul may be in Purgatory, but his body's up the road and there's cake and biscuits going. Now, will you look in the drawers for those beads?

ROSIE and APRIL vanish into the hidden area, stage left, as SEAN enters, causing ANNA to turn from the window.

● ● ●

SEAN: Anna, I called, did you not hear? It's some neighbour. I had to ask her in.

ANNA: (*Annoyed with him*) Why?

SEAN: What do you want us to do, hide up here in the bedroom? I didn't ask her to call.

ANNA: But you asked her in.

SEAN: She's a neighbour, for God's sake, with a present in her hand. I'd no choice. Beside I saw it on my parents' street too often, new people moving in, hedges coming down, walls going up, the time of day for nobody. We're not going to be like that.

ANNA: You could at least have waited. I wasn't ready. You had me half naked up here.

SEAN: Sure it was my last chance. (*Stuffy put on tone*) There'll be no more of that carry on when we're "residents".

ANNA: (*Appeased and amused*) Get away out of that!

SEAN: (*Taking her hand*) Come on now or I'll open the present myself.

ANNA: (*Good humour restored*) You will not!

SEAN and ANNA exit stage right.

●　●　●

APRIL and ROSIE run back into the bedroom from stage left, APRIL taunting ROSIE by waving a set of rosary beads before her.

ROSIE: Give me them, they're mine, give me...

The girls fall on the bed, briefly tussling again.

APRIL: I'll give you that grey scarf to cover your head, Piggy.

ROSIE: Don't call me, Piggy.

APRIL: Piggy, piggy.

APRIL: Does Mammy know?

APRIL: (*Hushing her with a fierce hiss*) Mammy doesn't need to know. We're only paying our respects to the dead. The man was your neighbour! Now you just look sad and kneel down to say a prayer for his soul like the rest of us or old Pointy Nose won't give us a thing to eat. Come on.

ANNA and SEAN have entered the kitchen to greet THE CALLER. ANNA stares at THE CALLER as ROSIE stands upstage, carefully positioned between them in the audience's sight-lines.

ROSIE: (*Quietly*) April, I'm scared. I've never seen a corpse before.

APRIL is suddenly conscious of being ROSIE's big sister.

APRIL: (*Soberly*) It's just... (*Excitement takes over*) Just think of the cake and biscuits, Piggy.

She exits stage right. ROSIE hesitates, stranded for a moment before following.

ROSIE: (*Exiting*) April, wait for me!

● ● ●

THE CALLER: I'm sorry for just barging in. You must have so many things on your mind...

ANNA: No, you're welcome. It's lovely to meet a neighbour, but I'm afraid we haven't any chairs to sit down on yet, except this old junk.

THE CALLER: I brought you this. I hope you don't mind.

She thrusts the bottle wrapped in brown paper towards ANNA who is pleased and a little embarrassed.

THE CALLER: Your first night, a settling-in present. (*Slightly embarrassed herself*) It's not champagne actually, it's sparkling wine. A bit like Babycham I suppose. Maybe you're used to champagne?

SEAN: (*Half-laugh*) Champagne cider, more like.

ANNA: (*Flushed with pleasure at the gift*) Never mind him. We'll be used to glasses of water after the mortgage on this place. But we've nothing to drink from. (*ANNA takes the bottle from the bag and shows it to SEAN*) Maybe Sean... the shop down the road... you might be able to buy three paper cups?

THE CALLER: No please, it's meant for you to drink, not me.

SEAN: But we insist. You're the first neighbour we've met.

THE CALLER: I'm not a neighbour.

ANNA and SEAN pause for a second, slightly perturbed.

SEAN: You're a friend of the Bennetts?

THE CALLER: (*Embarrassed*) I've never actually met them.

SEAN: The estate agents?

THE CALLER: Look it, this is just a gift. I saw the lights, I knew those other people had gone, I decided to buy it at the off-license on the corner. I'm sorry, it's foolish of me. I didn't mean any harm. Don't worry, I won't come back.

THE CALLER begins to exit. ANNA glances at SEAN, slightly annoyed at his tone. She looks at THE CALLER again, searching her face for a clue.

ANNA: (*Intuitively, handing the wine to SEAN*) It's okay, I know who you are. Men are slow. Maybe you'd like to look around the house again? There's nothing much to see with all the furniture gone, but...

THE CALLER: No, I'd be disturbing you...

ANNA: It's a nice gesture to call. No hard feeling.

THE CALLER: (*Tempted*) Would you mind? No, maybe...

ANNA: Take a last look. I mean it doesn't even feel like ours yet. I'm still only looking around it myself.

ANNA begins to exit, beckoning THE CALLER to follow. SEAN raises his eyes to heaven and gestures to ANNA to keep the visit short. ANNA and THE CALLER exit. SEAN follows and returns with a section of the new bed in a cardboard box. He kneels to reach in and find the instructions, then begins to study them.

● ● ●

While SEAN is so engaged, APRIL (in a different dress) rushes into the bedroom, flushed, with ROSIE chasing after her. APRIL is clutching an envelope which Rosie tries to grab off her.

ROSIE: Go on, show me.

APRIL: (*Climbing up onto the bed*) No, it's private.

ROSIE follows, still trying to get it. April holds the envelope up high.

APRIL: I said no. (*Her sternness takes on a teasing edge*) You're too young.

ROSIE: So are you. If Mammy finds out...

APRIL: And how will Mammy find out?

ROSIE: I could... tell...

APRIL: (*Menacingly*) You wouldn't dare, Piggy. What I would do to you...

ROSIE suddenly grabs the card from APRIL'S hand and runs shrieking to the top of the bed. Standing on tip-toes, she holds it up high as April tries to retrieve it.

APRIL: You little bitch, give me that...

KATE enters the kitchen, stage right, with a sweeping brush.

KATE: Girls? What's all the racket up there?

At her voice, the girls freeze for a second on the bed.

● ● ●

SEAN: (*Looking up from the pages*) Brilliant. The instructions are all in Japanese.

● ● ●

KATE exits. APRIL reaches up to try to grab the piece of paper.

ROSIE: (*Quietly*) I'll scream and she'll come up. She'll want to see...

APRIL: (*Vicious whisper*) Piggy... little bitch.

ROSIE: I'll scream.

With APRIL kept at bay by the threat, ROSIE perches up on the bedstead to unfold the sheet of paper. APRIL settles back, secretly rather pleased.

ROSIE: (*Reading off the paper*)

"Sweetie-pie, I am not married yet
You are not too late,
So write to me one line of love
And mine reciprocate.
'Twould be a heinous sacrilege
To die a maid or flirt
When it could be your privilege
To wash my flannel shirt."

She looks down up at APRIL, unable to surpress her laughter.

ROSIE: To wash his flannel shirt? I'd tell him what to do with his flannel shirt.

APRIL manages to grab the paper back.

APRIL: (*Hurt*) Well, you've never got a Valentine, have you?

ROSIE: If it's an offer to spend my life as a washerwoman I don't think I want one. It's no wonder you were hiding it. Wonder what he wrote on Betty Doran's?

APRIL: (*Vicious whisper again*) Bloody little bitch. Bloody bitch.

She strikes ROSIE across the head with her open palm, only half-playfully, as ROSIE ducks down with her back to her.

● ● ●

SEAN: (*To himself*) Bloody bed.

He rises, lifting up the cardbox box and exits.

● ● ●

ROSIE: Saying bloody is a sin.

APRIL: Bloody, bloody, bloody little sneaky bitch. I hate you. I should have a room of my own, not be sharing with a kid like you.

ROSIE: I'm only a year younger.

APRIL: You're a kid, I'm a woman. You're... (*She plays on the grandeur of the words with a put-on accent*) immaterial... essentially elemental... predominantly minuscule... I'll put you out on the street when I'm running this house.

KATE enters the kitchen from stage right and spreads a cloth over the table, then exits.

ROSIE: God forgive you. I'll tell Mammy you're wishing them dead.

APRIL: I am not. I'm just saying that one day...

ROSIE: It's a sin.

APRIL: Go back to playing with your dolls.

ROSIE: You'd want to join in. (*Chants, mocking voice*) "Patricia, Catherine, Jonathan, Thomas, Bernadette."

APRIL: (*Aiming a slap at her head*) Dhun do gob, Piggy.

ROSIE: (*Mocking voice*) "Look, baby Patricia, see the view from the window where your Mammy used to play."

APRIL aims another slap at ROSIE's head who ducks down lower.

APRIL: You're a sneaky little titch and I'm sick of you.

ROSIE: Well, beat me up on your own side of the bed, so.

APRIL falls back onto her side of the bed. She coughs for a moment. ROSIE risks glancing up and then lies back.

ROSIE: Your leg's on my side of the bed.

APRIL: Shut up, pest.

ROSIE moves her leg over to touch APRIL's, then uses it to try and push APRIL's leg across the bed. APRIL pushes her leg back and there is a sudden tangle of limbs as both try to push the other away. APRIL wins and pushes ROSIE out to fall onto the floor. ROSIE picks herself up, trying to recover her dignity while APRIL stretches out to take full possession of the bed.

ROSIE: (*Going behind the bed to stare down at the smug APRIL*) Did Mammy tell you about the present that arrived for you?

APRIL: (*Sitting up, excited*) What? When?

ROSIE: (*Coming back around the bed to savour the joke*) Some fellow with a big dickey-bow. He left you a large packet of Daz washing powder.

APRIL: Little bitch.

She falls onto ROSIE, starting to tickle the younger girl who shrieks with laughter and tries to shrug her off. They both fall out of the bed onto the floor, stage left, with the quilt on top of them. KATE comes back into the kitchen, stage right, her voice freezing them.

KATE: (*Calling up*) Girls, if I have to go up to the pair of you, you'll be sorry.

KATE exits. APRIL grudgingly releases her sister, and both carefully raise their heads to peer across the mattress at the door and listen.

ROSIE: Is that her coming?

ANNA enters the bedroom with THE CALLER lagging behind her, as if almost reluctant to step into the room.

APRIL: No. Sounds like next door.

ROSIE: Listen.

The girls rise and, clutching the quilt about them, back away so that they are out of sight, stage left.

● ● ●

ANNA: Not much for you to look in this room really. I don't think the Bennetts ever used it. It needs painting but there again we'll paint them all. I mean you don't like to think you're living in somebody else's colours.

THE CALLER: (*Touching the bedstead*) Will this be the child's room?

ANNA: We haven't made any decisions. (*Switching the conversation*) Have you many... yourself?

THE CALLER: No. I dreamt of them for years, but never...

ANNA: I'm sorry, I didn't mean to pry.

THE CALLER: It's okay, that's long in the past now.

● ● ●

Almost as if momentarily forgetting ANNA, THE CALLER watches ROSIE and APRIL re-enter the bedroom, throwing the quilt back on the bed and climbing onto it.

ROSIE: It's okay, she's not coming up. Who sent the Valentine?

APRIL: Not telling.

ROSIE: You don't know.

APRIL: Do.

ROSIE: Don't.

● ● ●

THE CALLER: (*To herself*) You just don't know.

● ● ●

APRIL: It's private. You can't know everything, sneaky puss.

● ● ●

ANNA: (*Puzzled*) What did you say?

THE CALLER doesn't seem to hear her. ANNA starts to feel slightly perturbed by her behaviour.

• • •

ROSIE: You can't call me sneaky.

APRIL: What do you mean?

ROSIE: Just.

APRIL: Just what, Piggy?

ROSIE: Just that a little bird told me that when the match was being played in the college last week Daddy's field glasses managed to sneak their way in here from their case on top of the wardrobe.

APRIL: And do you know what little birds like to be fed? (*She puts her hand to ROSIE's mouth as if forcing something into it.*) Worms. Big worms. (*ROSIE tries to shake her head away, squirming at the thought*) Unless they're good little birds and hop quietly into Daddy's bedroom.

ROSIE: (*As they stop playing and eye each other*) I'll be caught.

APRIL: Go quietly and you won't.

ROSIE: She'll hear...

APRIL: Go on... the match will be over soon. I dare you.

ROSIE: What if I get caught?

APRIL: You're a good little bitch.

ROSIE, with a glance at APRIL, begins to tip-toe towards the door and exits with THE CALLER's eyes following.

• • •

CALLER: (*Becoming aware of ANNA again*) But this really has to be the child's room.

ANNA: I told you. We'll wait and see. (*Almost apologetic*) It isn't always easy to plan these things.

CALLER: (*Quietly*) I know.

ANNA: It must have been a disappointment to you.

THE CALLER: What?

ANNA: Losing out on the house. You could have outbid us if you'd gone higher, we were stretched to our limit. Sean said there was a woman bidder. He did well to get it.

THE CALLER: (*Surprised*) I didn't bid for the house.

ANNA: (*Confused*) But I thought you must be... (*Suspicious*) I mean, why exactly have you come?

THE CALLER: I just wanted...

● ● ●

Unable to continue, THE CALLER distractedly turns away from ANNA to watch ROSIE re-enter, holding the field glasses aloft. APRIL grabs them and races to kneel up on the bed, gazing towards the window.

ROSIE: (*Indignant whisper*) I got them!

She pulls at APRIL's shoulder as APRIL raises them to her eyes and stares out through the window. They are frozen, heads close together. ANNA watches THE CALLER watching them.

● ● ●

ANNA: (*Uneasy now, feeling a need to fill the silence*) The Bennetts left that old bed. It could be full of fleas. We're not really moving in until tomorrow, but I just felt... get the worse over with... the first night. Maybe we'd feel more that the house was ours then.

THE CALLER: That takes time. But don't worry, you'll make it lovely, this room especially... just perfect for the child.

ANNA: (*More determinedly*) Like I just said. We've decided nothing yet.

CALLER: (*With sudden authority approaching ANNA*) But the child really has to be in here. That's what I kept thinking, watching the pair of you across in the Park... (*She puts her hand out to lightly touch ANNA's stomach*) just how perfect it would be to have the child in here.

ANNA: (*Moving back, unnerved at her touch*) Don't touch... What do you mean you were watching us? Perfect for what?

CALLER: Even the way the sun comes in here in the morning. And that view...

ANNA: You haven't even looked at the view.

THE CALLER stares at ANNA, taken aback at being confronted.

THE CALLER: I think I'm alarming you. I didn't mean...

ANNA: You want something, don't you? Nobody just calls to a strange house. You've been here before.

THE CALLER: There's a ramshackle shed at the end of the garden with a corrugated iron roof.

ANNA: (*Glancing towards the window*) What?

THE CALLER: And a laneway just wide enough for a car beyond it. You can see into the kitchens of the block of houses at an angle between here and the corner, and, through the trees in McCarthy's garden, the Gaelic pitches in the College.

ANNA backs away from THE CALLER and turns to the window, her eyes taking in all these details.

● ● ●

ROSIE tugs impatiently at APRIL'S shoulder.

ROSIE: Who are you gawking at on the pitch? Specs McDonald, is it?

APRIL: (*Indignant*) I am not!

APRIL is suddenly racked by a fit of coughing. ROSIE uses the opportunity to grab the field glasses off her and push APRIL out of the way. ROSIE peers through them. Despite her concern at ANNA's alarm, THE CALLER cannot help her attention being drawn back towards the kneeling girls.

ROSIE: Oh, it's Larry Keenan so? That awful Brother Michael from Monaghan is refereeing them. Did you see the cut over Billy Duffy's eye where he hit him with the leather? He's throwing the ball in again and they're jumping for it. Gosh, Larry Keenan must have had that same pair of knicks since he was ten. They're miles too small for him.

APRIL forgets her coughing and snatches at the field glasses.

APRIL: Give me them back, I wasn't...

ROSIE: (*Mock horror*) Lord between us and all harm! They've after ripping open, all the way down the back!

APRIL: Give me them!

She snatches the glasses from ROSIE who falls back on the bed laughing as APRIL scans the pitch through the window.

ROSIE: And he has "April Bright wash my shirts" tattooed down his bum!

APRIL furiously falls on top of her, but her anger dissolves into smothered hysterical laughter. They lie perfectly still as ANNA turns back from the window to confront THE CALLER who is smiling at the memory she is reliving.

● ● ●

THE CALLER: I haven't stood in this room for seventeen years. Never thought I'd get the chance again or could ever bring myself to. Oh, I knew I could have come here any Saturday afternoon when it was up for sale, among the hordes of people tramping around, but I would have felt such an impostor. The likes of me don't buy houses. People know that and they let you know they know. It takes a neck like old Pointy Nose up the road who came sniffing around twice the first time it was put up for sale. Hardly able to walk she was, but still prowling like a vulture when she'd no right to be here.

ANNA: And neither does anyone else anymore, except my boyfriend and me. I'm sorry, but it doesn't matter how often you stood here, this is our house now.

THE CALLER: And your child's to be.

ANNA: Can't you see I don't like talking about being pregnant?

CALLER: But I wish the child only happiness. Here... in this house... in his little cot in this room.

• • •

KATE: (*Calling, Offstage*) April!

The girls climb into bed properly and pull the quilt up over them. APRIL hides the field glasses by sitting on them, guiltily. They watch the door, trying to look serious.

• • •

ANNA: (*Calls*) Sean, is that you? (*Louder*) Sean, come up here, please!

THE CALLER: Don't be frightened. I really didn't mean...

ANNA: My child is none of your concern.

THE CALLER: Please... listen...

• • •

KATE: (*Calling, offstage*) April!

• • •

ANNA: (*Calls*) Sean, is that you calling? (*Louder*) Sean!

THE CALLER: (*Approaching, with her hand out again as if to touch ANNA's stomach*) Please, don't be frightened. I...

Unnerved, ANNA runs from the room. THE CALLER goes to follow, but stops at the doorway. As she backs away from the door KATE enters and surveys the room. The girls try to keep straight faces.

• • •

KATE: That must be very funny homework the nuns gave you, Rosie Bright. It could hardly be Irish that's so amusing. Is it sums? (*ROSIE shakes her head and rises from the bed*) And was that coughing I heard again from you, April? This cold is dragging on. (*KATE bends to tuck the quilt in around APRIL who uses the opportunity to slip the field glasses across to ROSIE who hides them behind her back*) Did I see you running into the house earlier without a scarf around your neck? How do you hope to shake it off if you don't even bother to look after yourself? (*KATE straightens up*) Did you light that candle like I told you? Your father will be asking, April. You know he likes you to remember little Peter's anniversary. Answer me, did you?

APRIL: (*Quietly*) No.

KATE: I gave you money to light a candle. It isn't as though we can spare it. You had to pass the door of the church. I don't want to hear excuses about how you lost it. What did you spent it on?

APRIL: It's in the pocket of my coat. I wanted to light a candle. I remember Peter...

KATE: Don't lie. You know you were too young.

APRIL: It feels like I remember him. I said a prayer out in the porch of the church. I couldn't go in. I had nothing to cover my head with. I was hoping a lady would come along and I could borrow her headscarf.

KATE: And what was wrong with your own handkerchief?

APRIL: I coughed into it. I didn't think it would be right.

KATE: Sure it's dark in the church. God wouldn't mind...

APRIL: It was... (*very quietly*) blood...(*She looks up, speaking slightly louder*) ... dark... red... blood.

CALLER: (*Moving forward*) Oh my God.

ROSIE has stepped forward in time with THE CALLER. Now KATE's glare stills them both.

KATE: Be quiet, Rosie. (*More softly*) I think I heard your father's bicycle. Run down, Rosie, you know he loves someone at the door to greet him.

ROSIE runs from the room (still concealing the glasses) as EAMON BRIGHT (a middle-aged man in 1940s-style working man's clothes) crosses the kitchen, wheeling an old black bicycle with a bag of tools on the back.

KATE: (*Stroking APRIL's hair*) Come here to me child.

ROSIE'S VOICE: (*Excited, unseen, offstage*) It's Daddy. Mammy! Daddy's home.

APRIL looks scared as KATE sits to draw her to her breast in the bed while THE CALLER silently watches them.

KATE: There was a time, April Bright, you would have been down those stairs. A war every night about who got to jump into his arms first.

APRIL: (*Timidly*) What does the blood mean, Mammy?

KATE: (*Soothing her*) It's not what you think, love. There was never any of that in our family. But you shouldn't be hanging round with that Betty Doran, her uncle... you've just a bad old cough, congestion on your chest. (*Turning her fear* *into sharpness*) You should be looking after yourself. (*Quieter*) I better go down to him.

KATE exits from the bedroom. APRIL rises and draws the quilt around her, cradling up part of it in her arms.

THE CALLER: Patricia.

ROSIE silently re-enters the bedroom and follows APRIL who exits stage left as she recites the litany of names.

APRIL: Patricia, Catherine, Jonathan, Thomas, Bernadette. (*Her voice becomes more grown up*) I'd not wash your shirts, Larry Keenan. I'd wash your mouth out with soap for what you said to me today. And then I'd kiss it.

As APRIL and ROSIE exit, watched by THE CALLER, SEAN enters the bedroom followed by ANNA.

● ● ●

SEAN: What's been going on here?

THE CALLER: (*Turning to them*) Don't be frightened.

ANNA: (*Scared*) I don't know why she's come here at this time of night, but I want her to leave now, Sean.

THE CALLER: Please...

SEAN: What's this about the park?

THE CALLER: I watched yous there for a long time earlier. You didn't notice me, I'm not someone people notice. The way yous were watching the house... like children play acting.

SEAN: Why were you watching us?

THE CALLER: Yous looked so happy... so much in love. I suddenly just wanted to say... how wonderful it was that you'll be bringing a child back to this house.

ANNA: Why do you keep going on about my baby?

THE CALLER: Don't get me wrong. I wish you so much happiness.

ANNA: If I had not been pregnant would you have come?

THE CALLER: My childhood was spent here, happy memories, good years.

ANNA: I asked you a question.

• • •

EAMON enters the kitchen, stage right, and stand by the table. He turns, seeing KATE behind him and produces a packet of cigarettes.

KATE: I'm frightened for the child, Eamon. So frightened.

• • •

THE CALLER: (*To SEAN*) I know I shouldn't have disturbed you. I just wanted to leave something... a token...

SEAN: She asked you a question.

EAMON silently hands KATE the cigarettes and she exits.

THE CALLER: (*Awkwardly*) I don't know how to explain... I just wanted to make you feel welcome in this...

SEAN: In our own house. We've paid good money for it. It don't matter if you lived here.

ANNA: We don't need your blessing or anyone else's.

As EAMON sits at the table, KATE returns with a pile of crockery which she sets down on the table. She looks at EAMON, waiting for a response.

THE CALLER: I really didn't mean to frighten you.

ANNA: (*Suddenly very unnerved*) Then stop looking at me.

THE CALLER: I'm sorry.

THE CALLER turns away and SEAN takes ANNA in his arms for a moment, soothing her.

● ● ●

EAMON: (*To KATE*) Alright, you can bring her again. It's just... this weather, coughs are two a penny.

KATE: The child is not right. You can see her getting thin. I can skimp on something, forget my fags for the week...

EAMON: No, you're a demon without them. I'll give you the money, you know I'm not mean. If the child is sick I'd give you every penny. It's just... I hate waste. She's been up and down to Doctor Donovan before. Bring her somewhere else. Byrne over in Fairview.

KATE: Just because Byrne's sixpence cheaper.

EAMON: That's nothing to do with it.

KATE: I'll make the money up.

EAMON: Byrne is a good doctor, experienced.

● ● ●

ANNA: (*Breaking from SEAN's embrace to confront THE CALLER*) Someone died in this house, didn't they? A Mr Bright. Your father, was he?

● ● ●

KATE: It will be the dispensary doctor next. Byrne's a drunkard, you know that. People trying to dodge work.

Annoyed, KATE turns and exits, stage right.

● ● ●

THE CALLER: Twenty-three years next September, 17th...

SEAN: (*Sharply*) Did she ask you for the date? Did she say she wanted to know?

• • •

KATE returns with more crockery that she puts down.

EAMON: I'll not have Doctor Donovan looking at my girls. A man that wouldn't give you a straight answer, or any other sort of answer, unless you'd money rolling out of your pockets.

• • •

ANNA: It was among the deeds, his death cert with the transfer of the house. I turned my eyes away quickly before the date could register.

• • •

KATE: (*Anxious*) If Doctor Donovan found out I went somewhere else behind his back...

EAMON: (*With sudden anger*) My girls are healthy and Byrne will tell you so. There was never any T... trouble with... on my side of the family. That Donovan... making you feel small...

• • •

ANNA: Don't you realise? I have to try and bring a baby home here. I don't want to know about death, not be wondering in what room, on what date...

SEAN: (*Drawing ANNA back into him*) That's enough now.

• • •

EAMON: Girls are thinner now, it's the fashion, not a pick on them. Prettiest girl out there on that street. Just look at her. Poor Rosie not a patch.

KATE: (*Feeling herself dismissed*) I'll get your tea.

EAMON: Give Byrne my regards.

KATE: (*Knowing that even mentioning the name hurts him*) We all said a prayer... for Peter.

EAMON has risen.

EAMON: He'd have been... (*beat*) you'll have the money. Every penny after my tea.

KATE, about to exit, stops to look back.

KATE: (*Very softly*) You'll say a prayer for April too?

EAMON and KATE embrace and KATE exits.

● ● ●

SEAN: I really think it's time you left now.

THE CALLER: Honestly, I didn't mean...

SEAN: Can you not see you're upsetting my wife!

THE CALLER: I wasn't...

SEAN: My wife cannot be upset...

ANNA: (*Annoyed*) Ah, for Christ's sake, Sean, she knows I'm not your wife.

EAMON turns and quietly exits.

SEAN: (*Totally flustered*) My fiancée and I...

ANNA: (*Furious*) Is that a proposal or something?

THE CALLER: Listen, I didn't mean to cause...

SEAN: (*Turning on her*) Will you just take your cheap fucking wine and go!

THE CALLER bursts into tears, leaving SEAN totally floundered.

SEAN: (*To THE CALLER*) I'm sorry, it's been a rough night, if we could have a minute on our own...

THE CALLER turns and quickly exits.

ANNA: What the hell did you do that for?

SEAN: I got flustered, I...

ANNA: Call me your wife?

SEAN: Ah Jesus, Anna, it's just a figure of speech, so don't start now.

ANNA: Was that you talking or your family?

SEAN: Leave my family out of this.

ANNA: You can simply ask her to leave. It's our house, remember.

SEAN: I just wish to hell it felt like ours. What does she want?

ANNA: (*Scared*) Do you think she could be one of these people who go around snatching babies... she might be casing the place?

SEAN: Anna, you have to calm down.

ANNA: There's something about her scares me. God forgive me, I think it's because she's barren...

THE CALLER enters the kitchen, still in silent tears and tries to recover herself.

SEAN: What?

ANNA: God forgive me, but I don't like her being near me.

SEAN: That's a terrible thing to say.

ANNA: I know, but it frightens me... maybe I'd be like her one day... still childless... poking my nose in, unwanted, a nuisance latching on to anyone...

SEAN: Talk sense, Anna. It's only a matter of weeks now.

THE CALLER moves back to the doorway, as if listening up the stairs.

ANNA: Last night I started thinking maybe I don't deserve a child. Maybe it's not physical at all, maybe... I don't know... maybe mentally I can't handle the thought of every moment of every day... minding her, being responsible. Maybe it's because I'm too scared, maybe it's me that's making my body do this.

SEAN: That's enough now, that's crazy talk.

ANNA: Is it? How do we know? I mean I'll just be all alone with the child in this strange house, knowing nobody here, with no sisters or mother to back me up.

SEAN: There's my sisters, and you know well that my own mother's only dying to help...

ANNA: It's not the same. With her I'll be under inspection the whole time.

SEAN: You will not.

ANNA: I can feel it with your family, they don't know what to make of me. Your mother, she doesn't even know how to introduce me to people.

SEAN: Who's fault is that?

ANNA: You see, they have it inside you as well. The pressure to become just like them. Your mother's house was such a novelty at first, all the nephews and aunts and nieces pouring in through the door, quarrelling with each other and making up. I was never used to that. I loved the bustle of it. But Sean, that house is like a fertility farm most Sundays. I'm starting to hate the sound of all those children.

SEAN: Five minutes inside the door and you're on your knees in the thick of them, like a big child yourself. Those kids adore you, Anna.

ANNA: But your mother and sisters, they think there's something wrong with me.

SEAN: There's nobody in my family thinks that.

ANNA: What if I make it three misses in a row, what will they think then? What will you think?

SEAN: (*Flustered*) I'll think nothing. I'll think... I think... (*Calmer*) I always thought we should have waited longer after the last time. Until you were more ready.

ANNA: I am ready. Jesus, I was ready three years ago.

• • •

THE CALLER turns to look into the kitchen where KATE enters stage right.

KATE: (*A good humoured scolding call*) April! Rosie! In for your tea now this instant!

THE CALLER crosses towards KATE, reliving the memory of her. KATE stands for a moment before her, then turns, moving away from THE CALLER to exit stage right again.

• • •

SEAN: Anna, we promised not to go back over the past again. It's that bloody woman has us at this.

• • •

As KATE exits, APRIL and ROSIE almost dance into the kitchen from stage left, circling THE CALLER for a second as they duck and weave around each other.

ROSIE: (*Teasing*) Larry Keenan was keeping a fair step away from you. You know the way boys do, when they really like a girl.

● ● ●

SEAN: Do you think she's gone?

ANNA: She has to be.

● ● ●

ROSIE: And they go all gruff and start pretending they don't even see her in a crowd.

● ● ●

SEAN: (*Starting towards the door*) Maybe I should check... apologise.

ANNA: Wait! Don't leave me up here.

SEAN and ANNA exit.

● ● ●

APRIL and ROSIE cross over to the table, where they start to set out the crockery KATE has previously left there. ROSIE works diligently, APRIL more absent-mindedly. In the background, THE CALLER watches them.

APRIL: I didn't notice.

ROSIE: And the big red face on him.

APRIL: I didn't notice it at all.

ROSIE: Well, I suppose if my name was tattooed on a boy's bum I wouldn't be looking at his face either.

APRIL: "Thin Arms wash my shirt."

ROSIE: God forgive you. Nobody calls you that.

APRIL: Like twigs in winter, I heard Betty Doran say. (*She holds her arms out for ROSIE to look at*) Go on, admit it, they're thinner now than they were six months ago.

ROSIE: (*Uncomfortably*) Get on with setting the table or Mammy will be cross. She's as cranky as hell these days. Greta Garbo has thin hands.

APRIL: Put yours up, compare them. Mine were always thicker than yours.

ROSIE: No, I don't like doing it.

APRIL: (*Trying to put her arms against ROSIE's*) Come on, I'll show you.

ROSIE: (*Upset but unsure why*) No!

She twists away and moves around the table so that it is between them.

ROSIE: You're saying that my hands are fat and clumsy and yours are all elegant. Leave me alone. (*Beat*) Anyway, if Larry Keenan didn't like your hands he wouldn't be hanging around out there on the corner still, making big cow's eyes over at this house.

APRIL: (*Delighted*) He's not?

ROSIE: I looked back as we were coming in. Now Mammy might let us listen to the radio if we have the table...

But APRIL has already raced off, stage left, just before KATE enters the kitchen, stage right, carrying a large teapot in one hand and a plate of buttered bread in the other.

KATE: Come on, quickly girl. Do you not hear your father on the stairs? Where's your sister?

ROSIE: She's outside. Can we listen to the radio...?

KATE: Outside? Talking to who? Boys is it...?

EAMON enters the kitchen, stage left.

EAMON: Boys... I looked out the window there and I thought it was Father Deasy I saw on the corner on a recruitment drive for young members of the Men's Mission. And Lord when I looked again who was in the middle of the big circle only my eldest daughter?

ROSIE tries not to smile as KATE is momentarily furious.

KATE: It's no laughing matter.

EAMON: (*To ROSIE*) You're slowing up, young missy. We'll never get you settled up in service at this rate.

ROSIE smiles at what is obviously an old joke as APRIL runs into the kitchen, slightly breathless. KATE glares at her.

KATE: You've kept your father waiting for his tea, Your Ladyship.

APRIL: Sorry, Daddy.

EAMON tries to look cross as APRIL goes over to give him a kiss, but he slips his arm around her shoulder and, in an old game, left over from childhood, begins to sing as they sway together.

EAMON: (*Singing*) "...I'm leaning on the lamp-post on the corner of the street, in case a certain little lady goes by..."

ROSIE has to run over to include herself in the song. EAMON slips his other arm around her.

ROSIE and APRIL: (*Singing*) "Oh me, oh my..."

EAMON: "I hope the little lady goes by."

KATE: (*Her good humour restored*) Come on now, the tea will be cold. (*They stop singing and sit around the table*) You got your father's talent for singing... none.

*EAMON begins to cut the bread and hand out slices of it, while
THE CALLER (who has mimed along to the song) watches
and remembers everything.*

EAMON: Do you know what it is I'm going to tell you? Those
new houses we're building up in Cabra. They have people
moving into them before the mortar's dry.

KATE: So you told me.

EAMON: There's one woman up and down to us every day.
This isn't right in her house or that isn't right. She's convinced
De Valera himself signed the order to shift her family out. She
has that big colour picture of him that *The Irish Press* printed
at Christmas, and she's always saying to me (*Woman's voice*)
"Sure you wouldn't have a few scraps of wood and a lick of
glass to make a nice frame for that." (*Own voice*) She came
down to the site today, badgering me to come up to the house.
Her young fellows, she says, couldn't make head nor tail of
the wooden toilet seat. They weren't used to them things at
all, they were making a mess standing up on it and the wood
only lovely. Would I unscrew the seat for her? "And will I
take it away?" I asked her. (*Woman's voice*) "You most
certainly will not. I'm after measuring it and t'will make a
perfect frame for the picture of Dev himself!"

*APRIL and ROSIE break into laughter. ANNA and SEAN enter
the kitchen and stop as if afraid to disturb THE CALLER.
KATE begins to pour the tea.*

KATE: Funny how the same thing happened to you last year
up in Crumlin.

EAMON: Amazing charisma the Chief has with women.
(*Beat*) Ah, but those new houses they're building now are not
a patch on this one. Solid Portland stone.

ROSIE leans forward to take a piece of bread.

KATE: Rosie!

EAMON: Now, grace.

The family bow their heads in prayer.

• • •

THE CALLER: (*Softly to herself*) Oh me... on my... I hope the little lady goes by.

ANNA: (*Whispered half-giggle*) She can't still be here.

SEAN: I really should apologise.

SEAN moves forward but ANNA puts a hand out to stop him from disturbing her.

ANNA: She's like a witch, going round touching things. (*Beat*) Do you think maybe we should knock?

SEAN and ANNA stand, watching the CALLER who is engrossed in watching the happy family scene at the table. EAMON breaks into laughter, looking at APRIL.

• • •

EAMON: You want to keep a greyhound?

ROSIE and APRIL: Yes.

EAMON: Which one of you will walk it every evening? (*ROSIE teasingly points to APRIL*) Is it your poor Da to be worn out circling the park over there. It's alright for someone like Padraig Keenan down the road who has a strong son. Sure Larry can bring him up along the canal.

ROSIE: (*Giggling, still teasing APRIL*) Larry.

EAMON: But the strength of them dogs, they'd pull the little arms off you.

KATE looks sharply at EAMON, almost superstitiously upset at any reference to April's arms.

APRIL: (*Persistent*) But you had greyhounds before.

EAMON: When I was a young fellow without a care. I was one of the first men this side of the city to race greyhounds. Before the dog tracks were even built. Out in the fields beyond Dubber. Old Jimmy Harold (*Amused, KATE throws her eyes at heaven at the mention of the name*) used to take the back wheel of his Ford and we'd prop it up with a few bricks. Two good long lengths of rope bound together and strapped around the axle with a dead hare tied to the other end. (*He uses his hands to describe the whole process*) Jimmy would turn the key in the engine and whooosh! The hare would snake across the grass on the rope with the dogs after it.

EAMON glides the slice of bread in his hand across the table towards ROSIE who darts back with fright.

ROSIE: Uhhh, it's cruel.

EAMON: (*Amused*) Not at all. Too many hares in the countryside as it is. It's in the nature of dogs to chase them. But I tell you one thing, some nights it was the most travelled corpse in North Dublin. Henry Ford never knew what he'd invented.

KATE: (*Coaxing*) Come on now, April, eat up.

EAMON: He came to Dublin one time, Henry Ford. Big reception up in the Mansion House. Out comes Alfie Byrne, The Lord Mayor. "Put in there," says Alfie (*EAMON holds his hand out*) "Shake the hand of the man who shook the hand of half of Ireland." "Well," says Henry Ford, "Shake the hand of the man who shook the arse off the other half!"

KATE: (*Furious*) Eamon!

EAMON: Ah, 'tis only a story, sweetheart. The girls will hear worse on the street outside.

KATE: Well, that doesn't mean they have to hear it at my table.

● ● ●

SEAN knocks on the door, startling THE CALLER from her reverie. She turns, embarrassed at being found there.

THE CALLER: I'm sorry, I didn't mean to still be here.

SEAN: I didn't mean to offend you upstairs. (*Something in THE CALLER's look makes him need to explain*) But it's just that we've had our setbacks in the past.

ANNA: (*To SEAN*) They're not her concern.

THE CALLER: I understand.

SEAN: Disappointments.

ANNA: Say the word if you're going to talk about them.

SEAN: Plans that didn't work out for us. That's all I'll say now.

ANNA: Why can you never say the word?

● ● ●

KATE: (*Cross, yet anxious*) April, you haven't even touched your bread. Come on, love, you have to eat.

APRIL: I'm not hungry.

● ● ●

ANNA: (*To THE CALLER*) I've lost two babies.

● ● ●

EAMON: (*Teasing*) That's the way with first love.

● ● ●

SEAN: Not babies... miscarriages...

● ● ●

ROSIE reaches her hand across to take APRIL's bread.

KATE: (*Snaps*) Stop it, Rosie!

• • •

ANNA: They felt like babies, they were real in my womb. They left an ache like babies.

SEAN: That's the whole point in moving, Anna. You can't upset yourself, dwelling on the past.

CALLER: She's bound to grieve, I know... you never stop...

ANNA: (*Turning to THE CALLER*) This has nothing to do with you. I don't care who you once were. You've no right to still be here. No right in the world.

Upset, ANNA rushes from the room. SEAN stares at THE CALLER for a second, as if trying to explain and then follows ANNA. THE CALLER looks after them and then back at the table.

• • •

KATE: (*Pleading with APRIL, almost in tears*) You have to eat, love. For my sake, please. Get yourself well again.

EAMON: (*Reassuringly, as if he were master of his kingdom, banishing all evil*) Sure, the child has all the time to get well. All the time in the world.

End of Act One.

Act Two

Scene One

Music starts as the lights rise on ANNA (still wearing her coat as if for protection) in the bedroom, seated on the floor at the end of the bed, and on ROSIE who silently works at wringing out clothes in a basin on the kitchen table. SEAN enters the kitchen from the left. He passes ROSIE who works in silent, dutiful concentration. He pauses and glances back, as if sensing something, then shrugs, crosses the kitchen and exits right. A moment later he enters the bedroom, carrying the plastic sack which contains the sheet, pillows and pillow cases. He puts it down behind the bed and looks at ANNA.

ANNA: Is she gone?

SEAN: Not yet. I told her to take anything she wanted from the junk in the shed and then go.

ANNA: Should I go down to her? But why should I? I mean it's our own house.

SEAN: We were rude to her. I feel a bit embarrassed.

ANNA: Who wouldn't be rude to her, calling to total strangers at this time of night?

SEAN: (*Seeing the humour in the situation*) She's probably a complete fraud, you know, like those women who scan the deaths columns and turn up at every funeral.

ANNA: (*Responding to his mood*) Well, if she starts any keening I'm off back to the apartment.

SEAN: Funny, the apartment seems that bit distant already.

ANNA: I liked it though. Somewhere like here, you'd always be looking over your shoulder.

SEAN: Any old house you'd be nervous at first. They all have their own sounds. It takes time to get used to them.

ANNA: In my parents' house I know what they'd hear. The bolt on the front door. That's what I remember as a girl when my father worked the night shift, the sounds my mother would make when I'd be half-asleep. Water running out of the sink, the clink of milk bottles and there'd be fifteen, twenty seconds... you'd know she'd be just standing there, looking down the street, thinking about him in that factory, I suppose, or you wouldn't know what, and then the front door closing and the bolt drawn across. A lovely snug sound, the whole world shut out. And then her slippers on the stairs and I'd pretend to be asleep as she'd stand in the half-light checking me.

SEAN: An only child in an empty house. I'd have found that strange.

ANNA: It was lonely I suppose, though I didn't realise it then. It made me feel special.

SEAN: You never talk about your mother, you know that.

ANNA: (*More guardedly*) There's nothing to say.

SEAN (*Gentle, coaxing*) I don't believe that.

ANNA: She wouldn't have approved of us living together.

SEAN: How do you know?

ANNA: There would have been rows if she was alive, all kinds of awkwardness.

SEAN: My own mother is the same age.

ANNA: Yeah, but your family's different.

SEAN: Morals were lax in the old mud hovel alright.

ANNA: You know what I mean. Raising a daughter is different. You feel responsible for them long after you shouldn't anymore. A mother and daughter, things are never easy between them.

SEAN (*Teasing*) So that's why you want a girl?

ANNA: Once it's born healthy, that's all that counts. (*She looks around*) Where's the wine?

SEAN: Downstairs, I think. I could use a drink right now.

APRIL silently enters the kitchen, passes close to ROSIE at whom she glances dismissively and then sits down, as though peering through an imaginary window and ignoring ROSIE's sharp glance of reproach.

ANNA: We're like children hiding up here. Not that I could ever hide, trying to skip school as a child. She'd always know, my mother, that I was under the bed.

SEAN: I can see you alright with your legs sticking out.

ANNA: They were not! She knew me too well, that was the problem.

SEAN helps ANNA up onto her feet.

● ● ●

ROSIE: You're suppose to be giving me a hand to wring these out.

APRIL (*Still gazing from the window*) Sure I figured you'd need the practice if you're ever going to land a man.

ROSIE: And what are you going to do then, whistle and his flannel shirts will come running?

APRIL totally ignores her and leans towards the window, making beckoning noises to an unseen cat. ROSIE labours away, increasingly annoyed at being left to do all the work.

APRIL: You know only too well I'm a better catch. They'll leave me this house. (*She calls*) Puss, puss.

ROSIE: God forgive you. Now will you leave Coffey's cat alone.

APRIL beckons the cat again.

● ● ●

ANNA: You couldn't fool my mother, putting your tongue on the radiator or blotting paper in your shoes.

SEAN (*Sitting on the bed to put his arms around ANNA*) Blotting paper?

ANNA: Some girl told me it was suppose to drain all the blood down into your toes, so that you'd faint.

SEAN laughs.

● ● ●

APRIL: (*Enjoying Rosie's discomfort*) Come on, puss, in you come. I love that ginger cat. He'll always be welcome here.

● ● ●

SEAN (*Moving his hand down onto ANNA's stomach*) You're going to have some job explaining blotting paper to this little muggles.

● ● ●

APRIL: You'll only be allowed to come with your unwashed brood and visit on Sundays.

● ● ●

SEAN: He's going to think...

ANNA: Or she's going to think...

SEAN: That her mother is something out of the dark ages. Blotting paper.

ROSIE stoops to wring out the clothes even harder, banging the basin. ANNA and SEAN look down at the noise.

ANNA (*Suddenly serious*) Is that her shifting around again?

They listen.

● ● ●

ROSIE: You shouldn't be talking like that... wishing them dead.

APRIL: Facts is facts. And Daddy will leave me this house. I'm the eldest, and besides... I'm his favourite.

ROSIE wrings the clothes even more fiercely, trying not to show her upset.

● ● ●

ANNA (*Her good humour fading*) What's she doing down there? I don't like her coming. It's like a hex...

● ● ●

ROSIE: It's unlucky to say those things.

● ● ●

SEAN: That's silly superstition.

● ● ●

ROSIE: You might be sorry.

APRIL: The cat will have more rights than you.

• • •

ANNA: I can't help it... that's something else I get from my mother...

• • •

APRIL: (*Calling softly*) Puss, puss.

• • •

ANNA: Even as a little girl... such terrible fears in my head...

• • •

APRIL: Come on in the window, puss, don't be afraid.

• • •

ANNA: Even now... they make no sense, but I can't shake them off. Waking up at night, afraid to let out my breath.

SEAN: The stitch will hold this time. The stitch is not the problem.

ANNA: What do you mean?

SEAN: You've been doing this since you came out of hospital, standing back, refusing to commit yourself.

ANNA: To what? A house I wasn't even consulted on?

SEAN: What if I had consulted you? You would have just vacillated until it was too late. You loved this house when you viewed it first, you were racing around like a bird collecting twigs. Now we can't stop our lives until you decide to live again.

• • •

APRIL is suddenly convulsed by a fit of coughing.

APRIL (*Turning to ROSIE*) Please, Rosie... will you get me a glass of water...

• • •

ANNA: Do you think her father died in here?

SEAN: It doesn't matter if they all committed hari-kari in the kitchen.

• • •

APRIL: Please, Rosie.

ROSIE utterly ignores APRIL's distress and APRIL, trying to recover, moves past her and exits. ROSIE crosses to look out the window.

• • •

SEAN: This is our house now.

ANNA: Except that it doesn't feel it, Sean.

SEAN (*Forced to admit*) No.

• • •

ROSIE (*Angry, almost scared, hissing at the cat*) Shoo, go on, shoo! You'll never get your foot in this door, shoo!

• • •

SEAN: Even in the solicitor's office, glancing through the names on the deeds, Bennett...

ANNA: ...and before him O'Sullivan...

SEAN: And before him Roseleen Bright, left to her by her mother...

ANNA: ... and then the mother, wasn't it, willed to her by Eamon Bright...

ROSIE anticipates APRIL's return and goes back to wringing out the clothes.

SEAN: ...and then the first deed between himself and the Corporation. You're right, suddenly I couldn't think of it as ours any more, of anyone owning it, beyond maybe Bright himself. All the rest, we're just passing through...

ANNA: No, it's ours, Sean. We sweated blood for that deposit.

• • •

APRIL returns, holding a glass of water. She sits up on the table beside ROSIE's basin of clothes.

APRIL: Don't worry, I'll give you money for the ad when the time comes.

• • •

ANNA: So we can kick her or anyone else out without needing to give ourselves titles.

• • •

APRIL: Respectable girl, RC, recently kicked out, seeks live-in position. Very experienced at cleaning, washing and scrubbing.

• • •

SEAN: Titles, eh?

• • •

ROSIE (*Cuttingly*) I wouldn't want to list the things you're experienced at.

APRIL: Jealous.

ROSIE: They would even make Coffey's tomcat blush.

Trying to disguise her hurt by ignoring ROSIE, APRIL turns away and looks out the window again, perplexed at the cat's disappearance. ROSIE sneaks a vengeful glance at her.

• • •

SEAN: That would have been too much to expect, eh? Even for the thirty seconds it would have taken.

ANNA: What?

SEAN: You to call me husband.

ANNA: Why do you need to lie to her? Why can you never just be yourself?

SEAN: Maybe because I'm not sure who I am anymore. You're so busy proving you're a free woman that you leave me stranded in this limbo.

ANNA: You know I love you, isn't that enough?

SEAN: Not for me. Not any more.

• • •

ROSIE sneaks another glance at APRIL searching out the window for the cat.

ROSIE: Has the cat got your tongue now?

• • •

ANNA: I never doubted you once, arriving on your pushbike with your plastic bag and your stupid grin.

• • •

APRIL: Go back to playing with your dolls, Piggy.

• • •

SEAN: Then despite all your suitcases, why do I still feel on probation?

ANNA: That's your imagination. (*She listens as APRIL is suddenly consumed by coughing again.*) Is that her down there?

SEAN (*Listens*) She has a bad cough if it is. I asked you...

ANNA (*Rattled*) Just get rid of her! How can I talk with some stranger tramping around my house?

SEAN: Alright. (*He tosses the instructions booklet to ANNA*) See if you can make sense of these. Otherwise we're stuck with this yoke.

ANNA (*With a shudder*) I'm not sleeping on that, for you or anyone.

SEAN (*With sudden vicious frustration*) No, you'll sleep to suit yourself like you always do.

They glare at each other before he exits from the bedroom.

• • •

APRIL has managed to stop coughing. She looks back out the window, seeing the cat now and beckoning it again. ANNA sits again on the floor at the end of the bed, lost in thought.

APRIL: Puss, puss...

APRIL BRIGHT

ROSIE sneaks up behind her and claps her hands, frightening the cat away.

ROSIE (*Triumphantly*) Go on, shoo!

APRIL (*Annoyed*) You go to hell, piggy. (*Turning to her*) You'll have to go somewhere anyway when I get this house. Maybe we can find you a small farmer. He won't mind your face being plain as long as your arms are strong.

SEAN opens the kitchen door and looks in, scanning the room for THE CALLER. APRIL turns towards the door.

APRIL (*Haughty, put-on accent*) Come in, Roderick, I have your tea waiting.

ROSIE (*Mocking*) Roderick! There's no one called Roderick round here.

SEAN exits.

APRIL: The name of a girl with her own house travels far.

ROSIE (*Cuttingly*) Well, at least you have the name already.

APRIL: What do you mean?

ROSIE: And a reputation that travels far.

APRIL (*Mocking but still hurt*) Uhh...Little bitch.

ROSIE: Out from the college field in all directions... loose... fast.

ROSIE resumes wringing the clothes out while APRIL glares at her with a deep hostility between them. THE CALLER enters stage right, carrying an old leather tobacco pouch which she puts down on the table as she passes the girls. She looks at SEAN who re-enters stage left.

● ● ●

65

THE CALLER: So much of my father's stuff still there after all these years... I can't believe it.

• • •

APRIL looks out the window, puzzled by the cat's disappearance.

ROSIE: Even the tomcat's avoiding you now.

APRIL: (*Climbing over the chairs*) Who'd look at you anyway, you plain little jealous bitch!

APRIL exits left.

ROSIE: (*Spitefully*) May your twitchy little twigs of arms fall off!

• • •

SEAN: It's mostly junk by the look of it. I don't think anyone ever used the shed. What did he do down there?

THE CALLER: A hundred and one things. After April... my sister... he could never settle to anything. Printing, welding... a dozen little businesses he lost interest in. Anything to keep himself locked away out there.

ROSIE lifts the basin of clothes and exits.

• • •

ROSIE: (*Softly, more conciliatory, offstage*) April? April?

• • •

THE CALLER: Will you get a skip?

SEAN: Sometime next week. O'Sullivan gutted the whole house by all accounts. But the garden's been wild for twenty years. I doubt if he ever went beyond the back door.

THE CALLER picks up the tobacco pouch again, watched by SEAN, and holds it up to breathe in the musty scent of leather and memory. KATE enters the bedroom behind ANNA. She has greatly aged and shuffles slowly towards ANNA on a walking stick. There is a lit cigarette between her fingers. She seems confused and lost, in a faded night dress. She is carrying the quilt.

KATE: (*Softly to ANNA*) Are you tired, pet? You have a rest there now till I make the bed up for you.

KATE fusses around, trying to fix the quilt onto the bed.

● ● ●

SEAN: The only thing Bennett ever changed was a light bulb.

● ● ●

KATE: (*Pausing in her work to look down at ANNA*) Those old hospital benches, you'd be stiff after them. Offer it up for the Holy Souls, that's what you have to do, April.

She smiles at ANNA who is oblivious to her.

● ● ●

SEAN: He promised me he'd clear out the shed before he left.

THE CALLER: (*Putting the pouch back down*) I remember promising Mr O'Sullivan the same. I hadn't the heart.

● ● ●

KATE: Your chest sounds better... congestion... this damp old weather.

EAMON (also far older, worried and exhausted looking) enters the bedroom in pyjama bottoms and an old vest and stands silently observing KATE.

● ● ●

THE CALLER: It's funny... my father's kingdom was that shed. He'd been dead four years, but I was still uneasy entering it.

● ● ●

ANNA glances up towards KATE, slightly perplexed but unsure why.

KATE: Wait till the Spring. Now you have that bottle of medicine the nun gave you?

● ● ●

ANNA: (*Unsure if she has heard something*) Hello?

● ● ●

KATE: I'll bring up some hot water and we'll try the Friar's Balsom. That will lift it.

EAMON: (*Softly, coming forward*) Kate, please.

KATE: (*Peering down at ANNA, her voice bewildered*) Don't just sit on the floor, child. Into the bed now, come on.

● ● ●

SEAN: If there's anything you want... before the skip comes. We can arrange a time when Anna won't be here.

• • •

EAMON: Kate, it's late, there's no one here.

KATE: (*Utterly bewildered*) April, will you not even look at your own mother?

ANNA slowly gets up from the floor, glancing around, uneasy in herself. She takes a few steps towards the door and stops, only a foot away from KATE but facing away from her. KATE watches ANNA in confused wonderment.

• • •

ANNA: (*Scared but unsure why*) Sean? (*She sniffs, and calls*) Are you smoking down there?

THE CALLER: I didn't mean to upset her. I had no idea.

• • •

EAMON: Kate, it's the middle of the night. Please.

• • •

SEAN: The doctors say there's a laxity in her cervix.

• • •

KATE slowly reaches a hand up to almost touch ANNA's hair.

KATE: (*Softly*) April, April love.

• • •

SEAN: You have to understand, the miscarriages hit her hard. She stopped eating, all her confidence shaken.

• • •

EAMON: (*Gently*) Will I phone Rosie?

• • •

SEAN: It was so hard to lift her, especially after losing the second one.

• • •

EAMON: Would you like that?

• • •

SEAN: Small things upset her... they remind her...

THE CALLER: Do I seem that much of a witch?

ANNA suddenly shifts forward uncomfortably, a hand subconsciously checking her hair as if she had felt something touch it. KATE lowers her hand. ANNA moves away nervously, over towards the window, glancing around the room.

• • •

KATE: (*Still staring at the space where ANNA had been*) April?

EAMON: You know that April's dead, sweetheart, these years and years dead now.

• • •

SEAN: I didn't mean... I'm sorry. It's just that you startled her, coming back out of the blue.

• • •

KATE: (*Turning to EAMON, partly returning to her senses*) How could I forget? I killed her.

• • •

SEAN: We're still a bit unnerved by everything.

• • •

EAMON: That's not true. We don't know.

KATE: (*Holding up the cigarette*) These fags killed her.

• • •

ANNA: (*Calling down*) Sean, who's that smoking down there?

THE CALLER: But you'll be happy here. And the child too. You deserve it.

• • •

KATE: (*Scared and confused*) There's someone moving about, Eamon. I hear them at night.

ANNA flicks off the cord for the bedroom light, plunging it into semi-darkness and begins to exit from the room.

• • •

THE CALLER: These walls deserve it.

THE CALLER turns from SEAN, staring about the kitchen again.

• • •

KATE: (*Looking around, frightened as ANNA passes*) Who's there?

ANNA stops beside KATE in the spot where she had previously stood, only now she turns so that she is face to face with KATE.

KATE: Who are you?

ANNA reaches her hands cautiously out as if feeling the empty space where KATE stands staring at her. KATE in turn puts her arms out as if to embrace ANNA, although neither of them make contact with the other. An Angelus bell is slowly bled into the soundtrack. EAMON crosses to flick the light cord back on again, startling ANNA who stares, transfixed by the light blub which flickers on. ANNA backs away, scared and then runs from the bedroom. EAMON turns around to find that KATE has now retreated again back in her own world. She shuffles past, as if not seeing EAMON, and moves towards the window.

KATE: April, listen. There's the Aenglus bell from the college. (*She calls down*) Rosie.

• • •

SEAN: (*Interrupting the CALLER's silent thoughts, anxious to end their conversation*) So if there's nothing else you want... maybe you might leave.... before Anna comes down?

• • •

EAMON: (*Pleading, putting a hand on KATE*) Kate, come away back to bed, Kate.

KATE: (*Ignoring EAMON, blessing herself and reciting*) "The Angel of the Lord declared onto Mary..."

EAMON: I'm phoning Rosie, it's her duty to come home. I can't mind you on my own.

EAMON exits as KATE continues praying.

● ● ●

THE CALLER: (*Looking back at SEAN*) This is how I remember the kitchen... silent... my mother sitting here... smoking... the evening paper unopened before her...

● ● ●

KATE: (*Genuflects*) "And the word was made flesh..."

● ● ●

THE CALLER: And my father out in that shed... hammering away in the distance... banging...

● ● ●

KATE: "Hail Mary full of grace the Lord is with thee..."

● ● ●

SEAN: (*Softly, anxious*) Please... it's late now, I'd like to lock up.

THE CALLER: (*Looking back at the kitchen*) Some nights I'd lie alone in that bed up there and I'd hear his faint hammering... one o'clock... two o'clock... he's building a glider I used to think.

A frightened ANNA appears in the kitchen doorway. Neither SEAN nor THE CALLER see her. She stops, uncertain of herself, trying to recover her wits after the fright upstairs.

THE CALLER: I'll come down some morning, the shed doors will be wide open... nothing left inside... this big wooden bird... all circles and colours... I used to half believe it... as if one day he could just fly away and escape from his pain.

KATE has stopped praying, as if surprised at finding herself in the bedroom. She begins to shuffle from the room.

SEAN: (*Sits at the table, drawn into the story*) What caused his pain... your father?

THE CALLER: The worse kind of grief. A loss I've never even been allowed to know. To have known you had once had a heir.

SEAN: Jesus... who would want to know that?

THE CALLER: At least the world respects that kind of grief, recognises it, tries to understand.

ANNA: (*Surprising both SEAN and THE CALLER*) As against pretending it doesn't exist.

SEAN: (*Rising to cross to her*) Anna, are you okay? You look pale.

ANNA: (*Gathering strength*) I'm fine... why wouldn't I be? I was upstairs. (*She looks at THE CALLER*) That room... the child's room...

THE CALLER: Yes?

ANNA: It has quite an atmosphere of its own.

THE CALLER: That's only because it's lying empty now.

ANNA: Are you sure? Be honest, please, tell me. Is the place haunted?

THE CALLER: (*Approaching her*) No. Not for you anyway. And even if it was there's one thing that would soon banish it. What I felt I could never give birth to here.

SEAN: I've asked you not to talk about this.

THE CALLER: (*With sudden confused infuriation*) But I want to! (*Quieter*) I have to... for years I've been dreaming of coming here... I need to tell you...

SEAN: (*Firmly, ready to usher her out*) I'm sorry, but we don't need to listen.

ANNA: (*Cutting across him*) Can't you just let the woman talk, Sean!

SEAN turns away, confused.

ANNA: (*To THE CALLER*) But your father had a heir. Your name is on the deeds.

THE CALLER: That was the cruelest joke of all. For him to have to settle not even for second best but for third.

SEAN: (*Turning back*) Men back then... it was all about having sons. They felt different about girls.

• • •

EAMON (now the same age as in first act) enters the kitchen, picks up the tobacco pouch (which THE CALLER has left on the table) and begins to fill the pipe he carries. An anxious KATE (also playing her original age) enters behind him and sits down.

• • •

THE CALLER: (*Glancing across towards EAMON*) That's the funny thing. He survived losing a son. It was losing a daughter that withered him up.

• • •

EAMON: (*to KATE*) I don't care what they said in the hospital, there was no lingering decay in my family... (*Taking a sudden sharp look at her*) unless...

KATE: What?

APRIL has entered the bedroom with a basin of steaming water to sit on bed, hunched over the basin, with a towel wrapped over her head.

EAMON: (*Tossing the pouch back down on the table*) Your uncle... the one who died up in Belfast?

KATE: What about him?

EAMON: Were you honest with me?

● ● ●

SEAN: (*Trying to regain control of the situation*) It actually is quite late now...

● ● ●

EAMON: Have you been lying all these years?

Ignored and feeling excluded, SEAN briefly exits out the doorway.

KATE: What are you saying to me?

EAMON: What did he die of?

KATE: (*Rising in fury*) There was no TB in my family, nor ever was and don't you try and blame... and there's no none now. Look at what you're after making me do... (*She sits again, shocked*) mention it... here.

● ● ●

ANNA: Losing two children, that must have been hard on them.

THE CALLER: Those were the times that were in it. They were never able to speak of it afterward, even to each other.

EAMON sits down across from KATE, both of them entrenched and silent.

ANNA: (*With understanding*) Or to you?

THE CALLER: (*Silently acknowledging that understanding*) Your husband is anxious that I leave now.

ANNA: (*Smiles*) He's not my husband.

THE CALLER: He is really. He's a good man, trying to look after you. (*SEAN re-enters and The CALLER looks at him*) I don't need anything from the shed. It should have all been dumped years ago.

● ● ●

KATE: Congestion, that's all April has. You get me some Vic tomorrow. I'll make a flannel poultice, put in on her chest, piping hot and that will shift it. So don't you go inventing things and your own family nothing to write home about.

● ● ●

ANNA: It must seem strange to you, the house being so bare.

● ● ●

KATE: What about that cousin of yours who went off to be a nun?

EAMON: That's nothing to do with anything.

KATE: Home with her tail between her legs after a year and then off getting married. What about the shame of that?

EAMON and KATE glare at each other.

● ● ●

THE CALLER: Even after all these years I wake up some times and for half a second I still think I'm home.

ANNA: Why did you sell up then, when your mother died?

THE CALLER: Sorry?

ANNA: (*Still feeling uneasy about the house*) I mean was there any particular reason to leave here?

● ● ●

KATE: (*Unable to contain herself*) Better for everyone concerned if your cousin had come out those convent gates in a wooden box.

EAMON: (*With fury*) That's nothing to do with... leave my family out of it.

KATE: (*In a fierce, slow whisper*) Then don't you go wishing things on my daughter.

KATE rises and exits, stage right. As if watching her go, THE CALLER crosses over towards the table as EAMON rises.

● ● ●

THE CALLER: It's hard for any daughter when her mother dies.

ANNA: I know. All the things you realise you never got to say.

● ● ●

ROSIE has entered the bedroom and looks at the stooped APRIL who cannot raise her towel-covered head from the basin.

ROSIE: Hallowen coming early this year, Thin Arms?

APRIL: (*Coughing slightly*) Leave me alone.

78

EAMON turns and silently exits from the kitchen, stage right.

• • •

THE CALLER: Not that there was much I could have said. My mother... she spent the last years of her life in hospital... knowing nobody... not even my father, and after he died... not even me.

• • •

ROSIE: No using your hands now, get out the trupenny bit with your teeth.

APRIL: (*Another fit of coughing*) Go on, leave me in peace.

• • •

THE CALLER: My husband, he wanted to stay here. But I said no, a fresh start, some new anonymous estate where you wouldn't always be looking over your shoulder.

• • •

ROSIE: It's still my bedroom too, you don't own the house yet. And I've to sleep in here with the stink of Friar's Balsom.

• • •

THE CALLER: Not that it made any difference. Maybe I'd waited too long, minding them here, thinking I'd be free to marry soon, wanting to make it up to them.

• • •

ROSIE: (*Rising on her tip-toes as if peering out the window*) That Larry Keenan is looking for some clatter if Brother Michael catches him out there.

• • •

THE CALLER: The doctors found out... they have polite words for it now and wonder drugs and treatments.

• • •

APRIL: You know I can't take my head out. Mammy said...

ROSIE: Walking over by the trees he is, bold as brass, with Betty Doran.

• • •

THE CALLER: I was sterile, infertile, barren.

• • •

APRIL: (*Lifts the towel, near tears, straining to see out*) You bitch.

• • •

THE CALLER: The praying that went on in this kitchen. The pointless, stupid praying.

• • •

KATE: (*offstage*) April, I'm coming up to check you now.

APRIL: (*Pulling the towel back down over her head*) Is Larry really out there? You're making it up... for spite...

ROSIE: And why wouldn't he be out there with Betty? Lovely fat hand on her to hold.

ROSIE runs off, laughing. APRIL pulls the towel off her head and sits for a moment in utter dejection.

• • •

THE CALLER: I sometimes wonder would it have made any difference... if I'd stayed here, if I'd faced...?

APRIL rises, carrying the basin and exits from the bedroom.

THE CALLER: (*Looking at SEAN*) I can see it in your face, I've annoyed you now.

SEAN: It's just that it's really not our concern.

THE CALLER: (*Moving towards the doorway to exit*) No. It was stupid of me. You have your own.

ANNA: (*To THE CALLER*) Wait.

SEAN: (*Surprised*) Anna?

ANNA: Stay, please.

SEAN: Anna.

THE CALLER stops, not knowing whether to stay or go as SEAN walks towards the table with ANNA following.

SEAN: (*Angry whisper*) What sort of games are you playing now? It was you who sent me down here, it was for your sake...

ANNA: I've changed my mind, right. We've to deal with this and that's it.

APRIL appears in the bedroom from stage left, carrying a cardboard suitcase and an overcoat. She puts the suitcase on the bed and opens it.

SEAN: Deal with what, for God's sake?

KATE comes in the bedroom door and approaches APRIL.

ANNA: I don't know... something I can feel here.

• • •

KATE: (*Handing APRIL a nightdress to pack*) Are you packed yet, pet? Bring one of Rosie's nightdresses as well. I know it's small for you, but sure you'll not be long in the hospital. (*APRIL puts in the nightdress and then puts on her overcoat.*) Tests for this, that and the other. Do you have Mrs Boland's Lourdes water? (*APRIL nods and closes the suitcase*) Mind Mrs Caffrey's case now, remember it's not ours.

APRIL begins to move towards the bedroom door.

• • •

ANNA: If I'm going to live in this house I don't want to keep pretending that the past never happened.

• • •

KATE: (*Watching her, helpless*) All this fuss over a little old cough. It will not be long till you're sleeping back here.

APRIL silently exits and KATE sits on the bed in fear.

• • •

SEAN: You're changing your tune now.

ANNA: I don't need looking after.

SEAN: Then why spend your whole life asking me to do it so?

KATE rises and exits also. ANNA and SEAN are so engrossed they've almost forgotten the presence of THE CALLER who has been watching APRIL and now KATE leave the bedroom.

THE CALLER: (*Calling, half to APRIL and KATE, half to herself*) April.

SEAN: What did you say?

THE CALLER: (*Turning to SEAN and ANNA*) April Bright. Would you not say that's a beautiful name?

ANNA: Yes.

ROSIE enters the the bedroom in her school uniform.

THE CALLER: Roseleen Samway, that's what I'm called now. There's no poetry there.

KATE comes to the bedroom doorway in her coat.

● ● ●

KATE: (*To ROSIE*) You'll be okay on your own.

ROSIE: I want to go with yous.

● ● ●

ANNA: Who was she?

● ● ●

KATE: (*Checking for the bus out the window*) You know children are not allowed visit the hospital.

● ● ●

THE CALLER: My sister. The girl who should have brought a child into this house. (*SEAN rises from the table, annoyed*) Years later, some young doctor...

She stops, uncertainly as if awaiting permission from SEAN.

ANNA: (*To THE CALLER*) Go on, I want to hear this. I'm not a child.

• • •

ROSIE: I'm not a child. I want to see her.

KATE: (*Turning*) Do your homework. The bus is at the top of the road. We'll be home in time for the Rosary.

KATE exits leaving ROSIE scared and alone.

• • •

THE CALLER: He told them that sometimes it was throat cancer.

• • •

ROSIE: Don't like being left alone here, don't...

• • •

THE CALLER: The symptoms weren't understood then... anyone coughing up blood, they just said TB.

• • •

ROSIE kneels beside the bed and blesses herself.

ROSIE: (*Earnestly*)

"Scared Heart of Jesus, Thy Kingdom come.
Heart of Jesus, may I love Thee and make Thee
  loved.
Sweet Heart of Jesus, be Thou my Love."

• • •

THE CALLER: My mother got it into her head... there was no sense in it... only older people got throat cancer... she was convinced that her smoking had caused April's death.

● ● ●

ROSIE: Sweet Jesus, forgive me... pride, covetousness, envy, anger... I never meant her harm. Thin arms... I never meant... the Devil was listening... let her have the house... I don't want it... I didn't mean... it was spite... I didn't know what thoughts could do...

● ● ●

THE CALLER: We were all convinced we were somehow to blame... torturing ourselves.

● ● ●

ROSIE: I'll starve myself... strike me dead, just let her be well again.

● ● ●

THE CALLER: You see, April was like a shooting star here, all laughter and light.

● ● ●

EAMON enters the bedroom and crosses to stand behind ROSIE.

ROSIE: "My Lady! My Mother; Remember I am thine own. Keep me, guard me, as thy property and possession."

EAMON silently rests his hand on ROSIE's head.

● ● ●

THE CALLER: Women on the next street... April, they'd call me, absent-mindedly, like they couldn't remember I'd a name of my own.

• • •

ROSIE: (*Half-scared by EAMON's stillness*) Daddy? Where's Mammy?

EAMON: (*Crossing to sit on the far side of the bed*) The new tin church.

ROSIE: It's dark. It'll be closed.

EAMON: The grotto outside.

• • •

THE CALLER: We heard them whispering about it when we were girls... what families it was in... every few months a child's coffin passing down one of these streets.

• • •

ROSIE: Daddy, when's April coming home?

EAMON: Soon.

ROSIE: She'll be well again?

EAMON: Coming home soon.

ROSIE: And she'll be well again, won't she?

• • •

THE CALLER: Lingering Decay. They seemed scared to even say the real name for it. "Lingering Dicky", that's what April used to call it. Herself and Larry Keenan with their heads bent together, laughing at the corner, keeping us late for the Children of Mary.

SEAN and ANNA have been silently listening at the table. SEAN glances at ANNA who seems transfixed by the story.

• • •

EAMON: (*Rising, going to the window*) Are you praying for your sister?

ROSIE: But she'll be well again? Daddy, I'm asking you.

EAMON: We'll all be here, together... a family again. The Brights... (*He turns back to ROSIE*) a nice name, I always thought... April... a pity it will die out.

• • •

SEAN: (*Rising, angrily trying to break the spell*) The death of children. At this time of night, in my girlfriend's condition. Is this what you've come here to put on our heads in this house?

THE CALLER: You make it sound like a curse. No. It wasn't that at all. It's something that I haven't got the words to explain...

• • •

ROSIE: (*Still kneeling*) Daddy...

EAMON: I don't blame you. I could have sworn you were going to be a boy. Only six months after we buried Peter. Do you know the name I was going to give you?

• • •

THE CALLER: (*Embarrassed*) It was silly to even try.

• • •

ROSIE: It's not my fault. We'll have children for you, April and I... boys.

• • •

THE CALLER: It's late.

ANNA: There's so much to do if we're going to stay the night.

THE CALLER: I should go.

ANNA: (*Impulsively as she rises*) Maybe you'd like to help me?

THE CALLER looks from SEAN to ANNA, unsure of how to respond.

• • •

ROSIE: Maybe I could keep the name... double-barrel...

EAMON: What sort of man would allow that... Protestant...

ROSIE: I could give it to the boys as a second name then, confirmation, or...

EAMON: There's no Saint Bright.

ROSIE: There was no Saint April either.

• • •

ANNA: We can't even assemble our new bed. I've a mattress to make up upstairs.

SEAN: (*Hurriedly*) I'm sure I can fix that.

ANNA: (*Firmly*) It's late. The old bed will do us fine.

Stymied, SEAN stares at ANNA, trying to understand what she is doing.

• • •

EAMON: (*Lingering over the name*) April Bright. From the time I was small... what I always said I'd call a daughter... a quirk... the priest didn't like it, but I wouldn't budge. April Bright...

EAMON sits on the bed and ROSIE rises to kneel up on it beside him.

• • •

THE CALLER: (*To ANNA*) Are you sure that you'd like me to help?

ANNA: Yes, I would.

• • •

ROSIE: Show me Peter's photograph, Daddy.

EAMON: Your mother might come in.

ROSIE: She'll be doing the fifteen mysteries.

• • •

THE CALLER: (*Aware of the friction between ANNA and SEAN*) Maybe I'll go on up and start so.

THE CALLER exits as SEAN and ANNA stare at each other. SEAN sits on the table with his back to ANNA.

• • •

EAMON: Next year he'd have been twenty-one.

ROSIE: She won't even know we've touched it.

EAMON: I remember when Peter was born... thinking... the pram in the hall... at twenty-one... he'd probably be taller than me... I'd bring him down to The Cat and Cage for a pint... a grown man at last.

●   ●   ●

SEAN: (*Giving vent to his confused anger*) Well, that's just fucking great, isn't it? A fresh start. Just what the doctor ordered.

ANNA: Let her be part of life here again. Just for one night.

SEAN: (*More quietly*) I can see you after all this, scared stiff on your own here. You know your imagination.

ANNA: I want her to help.

SEAN: Can you never make your mind up about anything?

ANNA: Why should I have to? You want everything to be so definite, cut and dried. Life isn't like that.

●   ●   ●

ROSIE: Get the photograph down, Daddy.

THE CALLER enters the bedroom and stands at the top of the bed, watching ROSIE kneel beside the bed.

●   ●   ●

EAMON: Peter... just six years of age... your mother pregnant with you. I could have sworn you were going to be a boy... the rheumatic fever... no way for any child to die... you'd hear him all over the house, breathless... the little fellow always breathless.

●   ●   ●

SEAN: One set of rules for me and another for you every half-hour. Till the next time you come running to me, frightened out of your wits about nothing.

ANNA: I took you as my lover, not my father.

● ● ●

EAMON: (*Rises*) That Doctor Donovan looking down his nose if the room wasn't spotless for his visit... just coming and going every second evening... lucky to get a grunt out of him... different if we'd a bit of money to rub together... he'd have talked to us then.

● ● ●

ANNA: (*Sitting at the table to take SEAN's hand*) Do you not see, it's important... what she's saying.

SEAN: It's not for us...

ANNA: No, but for her it is. The least we can do is listen.

● ● ●

EAMON: Nothing to be done but wait... his little coffin already made out in the shed. The priest said that God would send us a son... (*Abruptly*) I'm bringing your sister home, Rosie.

ROSIE: Out of that dark old hospital.

● ● ●

ANNA: A child died in this house. I know it.

SEAN: That was years ago. Will you think of your own baby, Anna? You were frightened out of your wits earlier on.

ANNA: My mother was the same, superstitious about the most crazy things. It's stayed with me... waiting for the sky to fall on my head. If I don't face up to those fears now it will just go on, into my own child, sensing that her mammy's always afraid. If a child died here then I want to know.

● ● ●

EAMON crosses the bedroom to stand upstage of the kitchen table.

EAMON: April wasn't in the hospital. There were bills overdue, I had told them that I'd find the money.

ROSIE rises, wrapping the quilt around her, alarmed.

● ● ●

ANNA: I don't want everything just brushed away.

SEAN: Like I do with things, is it?

● ● ●

EAMON: They moved her... never even told us... the South Dublin Union... not even a nurse out there... just paupers shuffling around in uniforms. You'll not stick my daughter in the poorhouse. I shouted at the nun... I... I mean... I wanted to shout at her.

During this last line EAMON suddenly steps across the imaginary line from the bedroom into the kitchen and sits in silent anger and self-disgust on one of the chairs at the table. ANNA and SEAN instinctively spring up from the table, glancing back, sensing something which they cannot fathom. ROSIE exits from the bedroom, stage left.

● ● ●

ANNA: (*Moving away from the table*) I have to go up to her.

SEAN: You're using her. This is just another way of getting at me. Who says that I forget anything?

ANNA: It's true. You don't feel things the same. It's different for you.

SEAN: What do you mean it's different?

ANNA: It just is. You've changed this last year... always calculating. I can't pick up a paper but you've been scribbing on it, mortages rates, repayments, tax relief, money, money, money. That's how you break everything down now.

SEAN: For us.

ANNA: (*Exiting out the door*) I have to go up to her.

SEAN: (*Calling after the departing ANNA*) I said for us. It's no different...

SEAN stops and turns, shaking his head in fury. He walks over to stand behind EAMON, placing his hands on the back of EAMON's chair, and bowing his head in an identical pose to EAMON. ROSIE enters the kitchen and tentatively approaches EAMON.

● ● ●

EAMON: I'm taking her home to be with us here, as soon as I've made a room ready.

SEAN sits, brooding, on the chair next to EAMON's.

ROSIE: It's clean, you know that I keep the bedroom clean.

EAMON: We'll clear out the shed. We can make it nice down there. Cut up the curtains from your room. I can knock out a window. Take the glass from the picture of the Sacred Heart. It's small enough, but it would let in light. Put in a proper window when I find the money.

● ● ●

ANNA enters the bedroom where THE CALLER is seated on the bed.

ANNA: Was this the room... where your sister lay?

● ● ●

ROSIE: (*Shocked*) You'll not put her in the shed, Daddy. What are you talking about...

● ● ●

THE CALLER: (*Rising, glancing towards the window*) No... out there... in the shed... after we knew how sick she was.

● ● ●

ROSIE: I can smell drink off you... she'll sleep with me, like she always...

EAMON: (*Rising*) The doctor won't allow it... contagious, he says... there was never lingering decay in our family I told him... unless your mother's... no... who gave it to her? What little coughing bitch down the street? I told your mother, that time there was no work going, don't be sending April down to Parnell Street for the broken loaves... every class of pauper spitting in the bakery queue... send Rosie... she never got it from us.

EAMON exits stage right, not even aware of the terrible insult to ROSIE, who, deeply hurt, looks after him and then follows.

● ● ●

THE CALLER: Back in 1974... my husband brought me to Tramore for our honeymoon. We were booked into a chalet in somebody's garden. They had the place lovely for us, but I knew, soon as I set foot inside it, why it was built. Even after all those years, you couldn't disguise those huts. Families

94

avoiding the shame of hospital. I told Tim, somebody died in this hut, I'll not sleep here. The woman said I'd insulted her, there was never TB in her family. We had to go home in the end.

During this speech SEAN has risen. He touches the back of the chair when EAMON sat, as if puzzled, then exits out the kitchen door. KATE enters the kitchen, stage right, in her good coat and hat. She takes her hat off and puts it on the table, blessing herself.

● ● ●

KATE: (*A prayer to banish pain*)

> Shall Jesus bear the cross alone
> And let the world go free?
> No, there's a cross for everyone
> And there's a cross for me.

She pulls herself together, lefts up and hat and exits.

KATE: (*Calling*) Rosie! Rosie!

● ● ●

THE CALLER: I shouldn't be telling you this.

ANNA: (*Sitting down on the bed*) Ever since I lost the first baby people are always sheltering me. I cried so much, I suppose. I just wanted my mother beside me.

THE CALLER: (*Sitting on the other side of the bed*) And she was gone?

ANNA: Eighteen months before I met Sean she was in for tests. A doctor called me over. I breezed after him... not a care. I mean, she looked so well. He had to keep saying it to me... (*Slow male voice*) "Cancer. A matter of months." My mind couldn't take it in.

THE CALLER: It's hard for any daughter.

ANNA: I keep thinking I'm over the loss of her, but it's only now that I'm really feeling it. I mean there are things you only want to hear said by your mother.

THE CALLER: I know.

ANNA: Other people, they can't say them to you. Especially after losing the second baby. And so you start believing there are things you can't face, so that finally any hint of death frightens you.

THE CALLER: My sister died a long time ago.

ANNA: But children still die today.

THE CALLER: (*Rising*) Not like April... not... here.

ANNA: I know, but the fear of it, it has me paralysed. I keep waiting to lose this child as well.

THE CALLER leans across the bed and puts a hand out to ANNA, although she does not actually touch her.

THE CALLER: It won't be like that. I promise you. (*THE CALLER draws her hand back and smiles*) Come on now, we'll never get the bed made like this.

ANNA smiles too and rises, taking off her coat for the first time. She picks up the plastic bag with the sheet, pillows and pillow cases and puts it up in the bed. THE CALLER and herself take the pillows out and begin to put the pillow cases into them.

● ● ●

APRIL and EAMON enter the kitchen by the door, wearing their coats. EAMON is carrying her case. KATE enters the kitchen stage right and ROSIE runs on from behind her and starts to rush forward towards APRIL. She finds herself restained by the firm hand of KATE on her shoulder.

APRIL: Hello, Piggy.

ROSIE: April.

EAMON leads APRIL across the kitchen, KATE making sure that ROSIE keeps well back.

APRIL: You keep to your own side of the bed, do you hear?

ROSIE nods. EAMON exits stage right and APRIL goes to follow him.

ROSIE: I'm saying a Novena like you asked. It's lonely in the bed without you. Soon you'll be back up with me.

APRIL looks back with a half-smile as she exits.

• • •

THE CALLER: He worked all night for three nights, my father did. You could hear him hammering all down the street. Nobody said anything, to him or to us. There were no children playing in the lane behind the houses. I'd never known it so quiet... marked out for hop-scotch... somebody's skipping rope that nobody went back for. In school, the girl beside me, her mother came down. I was moved to a desk on my own.

• • •

KATE lets go of ROSIE's shoulder.

KATE: Don't you be going out. I want you to run down to Mrs Caffrey with that suitcase.

ROSIE: Maggie Caffrey in school says her mother doesn't want it back.

KATE: (*Trying not to show her hurt at the insult*)You get things ready for the supper, do you hear? (*ROSIE exits, stage right*) And set a tray for April, I'll be bringing it down to her.

KATE exits after ROSIE.

• • •

ANNA has taken out a sheet and is folding it. THE CALLER turns towards the window, hugging the pillow as she remembers.

THE CALLER: That was the thing. I couldn't help but feel that it was me they wanted down there. They'd already lost one child and I'd failed to replace him. And you know, I think I wanted to be down there instead of April. Everyone on their knees praying for her, and that glow, that bluey-yellow pallor like she were made of plaster, almost like she was a saint already. All my life I'd been jealous of her and now I was even jealous of that attention.

• • •

ROSIE enters the bedroom in her nightdress and goes to the window. She looks out, raising a hand in a slow greeting.

ROSIE: (*Softly*) April... Good-night April.

ROSIE turns, suddenly conscious of being watched from bedroom door by KATE who has appeared there.

KATE: (*Harshly*) Get away from that window, it's not a peep-show.

ROSIE: I was only just looking out to...

KATE: It's rest the girl needs, not you gawking at her.

ROSIE: When can I see her?

KATE: You leave the girl alone. I'll take her down her meals, anything she needs. You're not to go out into the garden even, do you hear? I don't want any excuse for people talking.

• • •

ANNA: (*Glancing towards THE CALLER at the window*) How long was she down there?

THE CALLER: Almost until the end.

• • •

ROSIE: (*Near tears*) She's my sister.

KATE: Quarantine, that's what the doctors said. We had to fight to get her out of that... poorhouse. And you'll give them no grounds to put her back in or I'll have your Daddy take his belt to you. Do you hear me now? Do you?

ROSIE: Yes, Mammy.

KATE: It's prayer she needs. Do you ever get on your knees at all, do you? Now don't you go near that window again.

ROSIE kneels at the end of the bed and begins to silently pray.

EAMON: (*Angrily, offstage*) Go on, clear off outa that! I won't tell you again.

At the sound of his voice KATE runs from the room in alarm.

• • •

THE CALLER: (*Turning back to ANNA*) It was madness. Don't worry. She died elsewhere. A ward full of girls saying novenas. Musical beds. Everybody moved up one bed when somebody died. Children counting the number of beds to go before their turn came to die.

SEAN has entered the bedroom and gives THE CALLER a sharp glance as he overhears the words.

ANNA: (*Not bothering to look up*) Sean, where is the duvet?

SEAN: Downstairs.

ANNA: Get it, will you.

SEAN: (*With an edge in his voice*) It's downstairs.

THE CALLER detects the tension in his voice.

THE CALLER: I'll get it, shall I?

SEAN does not reply.

ANNA: Wait, Sean can get it.

SEAN: (*Firmly*) It's in the hallway.

There is silence until THE CALLER exits.

ANNA: (*Annoyed*) There was no need for that.

SEAN: She's in the way here.

ANNA: She's not in the way.

SEAN: I want to talk to you.

ANNA: Later.

SEAN: Now.

ANNA: Now is not a good time.

SEAN: For you there's never a good time. Stop running away.

ROSIE blesses herself, rises and exits from the bedroom.

ANNA: (*With an anxious glance towards the door*) She'll be up in a moment...

SEAN begins to almost violently roll up the old horsehair mattress and pull it off the bed. EAMON enters the kitchen stage right, slams a stick down on the table for a second, picks it up again and exits, stage left.

SEAN: All those nights after we lost the babies, you in the bed crying... what was it you called me?

ANNA: I don't see what that...

KATE enters the kitchen, stage right, frightened and looks towards where EAMON has exited.

SEAN: Your rock. Your strength. Your shoulder.

ANNA: So you were.

● ● ●

EAMON re-enters the kitchen from stage left, still holding the stick and looks at KATE.

EAMON: (*Trying to calm himself*) Stones they're throwing now. Saying it might be all right down the country, but we can't use our own shed like that here.

KATE: Come in, come in! People will see.

EAMON ignores her and exits, stage right, again.

● ● ●

SEAN: (*Starting to exit, stage right, carrying the old mattress*) Did you ever think to look up from my shoulder, to look at my face... to see my tears.

● ● ●

EAMON re-enters the kitchen, stage right.

EAMON: It's my garden... my shed... I'll show them. Even if I have to sleep out in that laneway with a stick.

KATE: For God's sake!

EAMON exits again, stage left.

● ● ●

SEAN returns stage right carrying a new mattress wrapped in plastic.

ANNA: You never cried.

SEAN: Never in front of you. The cold boiler house sitting on a concrete block, or at night walking home with milk from the shops. Did you ever think to look?

●　●　●

EAMON re-enters the kitchen, stage left.

EAMON: I'll break this across the back of the first one...

He slams the stick down on the table. SEAN has carried the mattress to the far side of the bed. He stands it up and leans on it.

●　●　●

ANNA: I didn't think to. I was just so down, I'd no reason...

●　●　●

KATE: Maybe they're right, Eamon. She needs light and air.

●　●　●

SEAN: (*Tearing the plastic off the mattress*) "Be strong for me," you said, "if you break down I couldn't take it." That was the role you gave me, the only role you allowed me. The strong arm to lean on, the tough man who would look towards the future. I felt everything. They were my children we lost too.

●　●　●

EAMON: This is her home.

● ● ●

ANNA: It wasn't my fault that I lost them.

SEAN: You see. I open my mouth, I can't win. I never said it was.

● ● ●

KATE: People are frightened, the gardens are all empty.

EAMON: Just congestion she has...

● ● ●

ANNA: You never showed real grief. It's the way you're made.

SEAN: (*Putting the new mattress down onto the bed*) It's the way you made me. But just for once what about my pain? People in work, people on the street, it was all poor Anna's pain, all about Anna's grief. When do I get the chance to show grief?

● ● ●

EAMON: There was never anything in our families.

● ● ●

SEAN: I'm petrified by all this waiting... I'm even more frightened than you are.

● ● ●

KATE: God is good. It would be a sin for us to question his ways. You'll let me ask the priest.

EAMON: (*In self-disgust as he sits down, wearily*) The priest.

• • •

SEAN: (*Sits on the new mattress*) I wake up at night, the bed is empty, you're gone out to the toilet. I'm lying awake, I don't know what's happening. Are you okay...? Is it another...? (*He rises*) I can't even use the word.

• • •

EAMON: This is her home. She belongs with us here.

• • •

SEAN starts to put the sheet on and ANNA helps him.

SEAN: I can't pray anymore, I can't count sheep, so I count money. Just to control my fear. Mortgages, repayments, concrete things I can handle, that I can give you, things I'm allowed to talk about.

• • •

KATE: Father Deasy will know what's right.

• • •

SEAN: Men's things. The strong man, Sean, the provider.

ANNA: I work as hard as you, you know.

SEAN: Yes. You can have a foot in both camps, so why can't I?

ANNA sits, resting on the bed.

• • •

EAMON: The priest will just tell us to get Doctor Donovan. That man back in here again, looking down his nose at us like when Peter... I have my pride... I...

• • •

SEAN sits across from her on the bed.

SEAN: (*Quietly, suddenly revealing his fear*) Anna? Did they say anything else to you that last time in the hospital? Are you sure this baby will be alright?

ANNA: (*Frightened*) You always said that you were sure of this one, you were always so certain.

• • •

KATE: (*Softly, sitting across from EAMON*) People are mocking us, Eamon. And they're scared.

• • •

SEAN: (*Rises*) I just don't know. All these terms... cervical incompetancies and engaged fetal this and that... I try to follow them, but I'm trapped here on the outside... I just don't know anymore.

• • •

EAMON: (*Rises*) Doctor Donovan watched Peter die. Coming and going... not a word out of him... like the boy's dying was a nuisance.

• • •

ANNA: You're frightening me now.

SEAN stands at the top of the bed, both him and ANNA momentarily lost in their own thoughts and fears.

• • •

KATE: It would be wrong to cross the doctor. We'll need him at the end.

EAMON: Don't say it.

KATE: Pride won't save her. We need to pray... all of us... and when the time comes to accept death willingly from the Hand of God.

EAMON: She'll not go from her home till she has to.

KATE blesses herself, EAMON follows suit. They kneel beside the table in prayer. ROSIE enters the kitchen doorway, in her overcoat and hat, adjusting the prominent black armband on her sleeve. She walks slowly, drained and bereft. As EAMON and KATE bless themselves again and rise, APRIL steps out from behind the door, initially unseen by ROSIE, with a bright light creating a sense of radiance around her. ROSIE turns and APRIL holds her arms out, looking down at them in awe.

• • •

APRIL: (*Voice wonder-struck*) Look Rosie, my arms are no longer thin.

ROSIE: (*Awe-struck*) April?

APRIL lowers her arms and retreats back offstage with the light dying around her. ROSIE runs to the door.

ROSIE: (*Exhilarated*) Mammy, Mammy...

KATE: (*offstage*) What is it?

ROSIE: I've just seen... (*She realises she will not be believed*) It's nothing.

ROSIE takes one last look back into the kitchen and then, with a flush of joy, she exits. THE CALLER enters the bedroom, carrying a quilt in a plastic sack, rousing SEAN and ANNA from their thoughts.

• • •

THE CALLER: Just wait till you see the sun coming in here... a beautiful room for a child.

SEAN: (*Taking the bag off her*) Jesus, do you ever stop?

THE CALLER: (*To SEAN*) Nobody ever died in this room, if that's what you're worried about. (*To ANNA*) My father died downstairs after coming home from visiting my mother. In the time that it took me to go for milk. My little brother, Peter... the main bedroom inside... rheumatic fever... before I was born. April... there's nobody born on this street could ever forget April. Peter... I doubt if there's a soul left who remembers him. They were terrible moments here, but you see... this is what I really wanted to tell you. That I can't ever see this house as a sad place. There are too many good things, skipping ropes in the garden, makeshift grottos every May in the hedge of the lane. This was a house of such happiness.

SEAN has taken the new quilt out and folds it over the iron bedstead to form a rest for ANNA's back.

SEAN: It's nothing to do with us. We just picked the house at random.

THE CALLER: When I saw you in the park, I felt sure it had picked you.

SEAN: That's crazy talk.

THE CALLER: That's what I've felt for years. That this house has been waiting, longing for someone like yous. Your child... (*She touches her breast softly*) in here I know it. Your child will be born safely here.

• • •

KATE enters the kitchen, her face strained, her body a tight ball of tension. She carries a tray which she places down on the table and a suitcase which she sets down on a chair. ROSIE, in her school uniform, runs into the kitchen and crosses over, worried, to join KATE.

ROSIE: Where's Daddy gone running?

KATE: For the priest.

● ● ●

ANNA: (*Glancing at THE CALLER*) How can you be sure?

● ● ●

ROSIE: Has she's taken a turn? I want to go out to her...

KATE: (*Harshly*) You've done enough damage... dragging her upstairs.

She snaps the suitcase open on the chair.

● ● ●

THE CALLER: Because even the longest wait has to end.

● ● ●

KATE: What do we do?

ROSIE: What?

● ● ●

THE CALLER: Can't you see? There was so much joy held between these walls.

● ● ●

KATE: Things to do. You stupid girl. List them! What would happen if your father or I fell ill? How do we prepare for the priest's visit?

● ● ●

THE CALLER: Children's voices day and night in that lane. Children played here, were happy here once.

● ● ●

ROSIE: I want to go out to see April.

KATE: Tell me, you heathen!

● ● ●

THE CALLER: April, I can see her still, at the bend of those stairs, running down into a beam of evening light.

● ● ●

Fighting back tears, ROSIE takes a white cloth from the suitcase and fixes it neatly over the tray.

ROSIE: (*Trying to remember*) Do not keep the Priest waiting, but have everything ready for him. When he arrives, remembers that he carries Our Lord with him, and do not speak unless it is necessary...

KATE: Before that, stupid girl!

● ● ●

THE CALLER: If you only knew all the futures we lived out here... all the mornings when we lay... my sister and me... in bed here...

● ● ●

ROSIE: Make the room clean and tidy. Make the patient clean and tidy. Wash her carefully out of respect for the Holy Oil. Place a table a short distance away.

● ● ●

THE CALLER: The pair of us quarrelling, laughing, dreaming of the future... of our husbands-to-be... the lists of boys' names... lists of girls.

● ● ●

KATE: With what on the table?

As ROSIE lists the items she takes each one she can remember from the case and arranges them in order on the tray.

ROSIE: (*Trying not to break down*) With... with... a crucifix in the centre, then candles... two... flowers... if you have any... then... then...

● ● ●

THE CALLER: Which of us would marry first? Who would have a home with plastic roses in the window, with Venetian blinds and a husband who loved us.

● ● ●

KATE: Then what?

ROSIE: A glass... holy... no ordinary water, a teaspooon, for the priest to give the patient a drink if necessary, then holy water and... and...

● ● ●

THE CALLER: Who would walk up this street first as a mother wheeling a pram. Neighbours coming out to their gates, the pride we'd feel.

* * *

KATE: (*With rising fury*) And?

ROSIE: And... I don't know... can't remember... (*She reaches into the case a last time*) a brush, something to sprinkle it with, then... then... then... I don't know...

KATE snaps and suddenly strikes ROSIE across the face.

KATE: She's your sister and you don't know. Your sister dying and you don't know. After you dragging her up those stairs. Your Daddy should have beaten you harder. You...

* * *

THE CALLER: And we vowed we wouldn't be cowed like our mothers were, we wouldn't be churched after giving birth, we wouldn't need to be cleansed by any priest or anyone.

* * *

A deeply shocked and hurt ROSIE holds a hand up to her face, then bends to take the last item out. Behind ROSIE's back KATE puts her arm out as if to place it in apology on ROSIE's shoulder, but finds herself unable to do so.

KATE: The priest is coming. She'll be moved if she lives. Prepare the room.

KATE closes the case, lifts it up and exits, stage right. ROSIE lifts up the tray and carefully follows.

* * *

THE CALLER: (*To ANNA*) It would be a new world and we lived every day of it in advance, in whispers, in bed in this room.

SEAN arranges the pillows behind ANNA's back as ANNA sits down to rest on the bed. SEAN stands behind her, leaning over the bedstead to take her hand.

THE CALLER: So many life-times ago. And now look at you here at last... your stomach ripe for birth... these walls... don't be frightened, please... that's all I've really came to say... that for years I've felt these walls have been aching to hear a baby shifting in his sleep, banging his feet against the bars of a cot. It's a good room for a child this... my cot stood by that window... the cot my father made in that shed... the cot April lay in before me and Peter before her. But I want you to know... there are no ghosts here, just longings that are left over. And when you bring your child home even they will be banished for ever.

ANNA: And you're sure it will be born safely?

THE CALLER: May God dry up my... (*Stops*) I swear.

ANNA: April. It's not a name I'd ever think of calling...

THE CALLER: And why would you? It's the future you've got to be thinking of now. The bed is made. I'd like to go please.

ANNA rises from the bed and holds her hand out to THE CALLER.

ANNA: Thank you for the present... and thank you for calling.

THE CALLER smiles and reaches over to briefly touch ANNA'S fingers and hold them against ANNA'S stomach.

SEAN: We'll see you down.

● ● ●

*THE CALLER exits with SEAN and ANNA following. After
they have gone ROSIE enters the bedroom, stage left, helping
APRIL (who is in a dressing gown with their old quilt around
her shoulders) to sit on the bed and get her breath back.*

APRIL: Daddy will beat you black and blue, you know that?

ROSIE: Don't care. I watched to see where he kept the key.

APRIL: Don't know if I'm strong enough to get back down
again.

ROSIE: I'll not have you locked away out there.

APRIL: Some nights I hear boys come to the edge of the lane.
They shout things... cruel... men coming home from the pub,
doing their business, the sound of them. You know Coffey's
ginger cat... Daddy leaves the window open... some nights he
actually comes in if it's cold, looking for warmth. Once he
brought in a dead bird. (*Looks around*) So little sound in the
day-time... footsteps, and when they get close they start to run.
How are the nuns, Piggy?

*ROSIE kneels up on the bed behind APRIL and puts her arms
around APRIL's shoulder.*

ROSIE: How are they ever?

APRIL: I'd love to go for a drive in a car. Do you think will
I ever...?

ROSIE: Of course you will.

APRIL: In a box...

ROSIE: Don't say that! Don't ever! What sort of God would
let that happen?

APRIL: They were playing football in the College last week.
It must have been a wild shot, the ball landed in the lane. I
heard the whistle, somebody climb over. I knew it was Larry
Keenan, that he'd kicked it wide on purpose. I heard him drop
down, pick up the ball, and the way he stood there, outside
the shed door... I could almost hear him breathing. What could
he say? I knew it was him and I was lying there just in my

113

nightdress. And I could hear the Christian Brother shouting for him to hurry up... and it was like... I don't know... I just felt he had his cheek pressed against the door. All the times I wouldn't let him kiss me... then I heard the ball being kicked back, boots climbing, and I knew he'd never come again.

APRIL falls silent.

● ● ●

ANNA and SEAN enter the kitchen.

SEAN: Of all the strange visitors. I could use a drink. (*He glances under the table*) Where did she put that wine?

ANNA: Sean, did you really cry all those times?

SEAN: (*Sitting down*) Yes.

ANNA comes to stand in front of him and SEAN puts his arms around her.

ANNA: You know, you'd never believe how lonely I was, all those years until I found you. All those grubby men down in Sack's Nightclub. And yet, that time, taking the taxi across to the apartment, I almost didn't move in with you. Did I ever tell you that?

SEAN: No.

ANNA: (*Sits as well*) I used to wonder would I be better off by myself, never having to be frightened of losing somebody again? I didn't know if I'd have the strength to go through that. (*She looks down at her stomach*) Look at me now and I still don't know... the strength to marry... to commit myself... knowing it will end... but that's part of it, eh? In sickness and in health.

SEAN reaches across to take her hand.

● ● ●

APRIL: Mammy says she won't smoke down in the shed. I know she's not smoking in the house either. They're saving for the funeral. So Old Pointy Nose can have her revenge. Tea and cake at my expense.

APRIL is consumed by a violent fit of coughing. She clutches a pillow to her chest and spits up into a handkerchief. ROSIE climbs off the bed, a little scared and crosses to check out the window.

● ● ●

SEAN: We don't need no priest to tell us that. (*Beat*) Anna, we'll be happy here, I promise you.

ANNA: I know we will. (*She rises*) I'll go on up, tomorrow's moving in day.

SEAN: Do you think she'll ever come again?

ANNA: No. (*She begins to exit, calling back*) Sean, don't forget to check the bolt on the back door.

SEAN: I won't. (*He checks around again*) She did bring a bottle of wine, didn't she?

SEAN exits stage right as if to check the back door. APRIL rises with the quilt around her and joins ROSIE.

● ● ●

APRIL: So many things to remember. To sleep with my hands across my breast, to pray to accept, with willingness and resignation, whatever manner of death it may please Our Lord to send me.

SEAN enters the kitchen again, crosses the stage, switches off the light and exits, closing the kitchen door.

ROSIE: Stop it, April. I'm praying for you, we're all praying. When spring comes, wait till you see how much better you'll feel. I don't want the house, April. May God strike me barren, may he dry up my womb before a child of mine runs up these stairs. Remember the games we used to play here.

APRIL: Silly... childish.

ROSIE: Patricia, Catherine, Jonathan, Thomas, Bernadette.

APRIL: Stupid, tempting faith.

ROSIE: No. You'll hold them all at this window one day. Play the game for me, just once.

ANNA silently enters the bedroom and fingers the bedstead lightly, lost in her own throughts. APRIL, a little unsteady, folds part of the quilt up to form the shape of a child in her arms and looks out the window.

APRIL: (*Surrendering herself to the game*) Look out there, little Baby Jonathan. There's the garden your mother used to play in.

ROSIE: Patricia. You said the first one would be a girl, Patricia.

APRIL: (*Looks down*) What? Crying. Baby's hungry. (*Drawn out of the fantasy*) Even my breasts are thin.

ROSIE: (*Urgently*) Feed him, April. You will feed him. And Patricia and Catherine and Thomas and Bernadette. And you'll live here and I'll come to visit, week in and week out, and we'll drink coffee by then and not tea.

● ● ●

ANNA looks up as SEAN enters the bedroom.

ANNA: Just ten more weeks and yet, you know, sometimes it still feels as unreal as when I was a girl playing with dolls.

● ● ●

APRIL: (*Drawn back into the fantasy*) He has his daddy's eyes...

• • •

SEAN: (*Spreading the new duvet properly over the bed*) It will be real alright. I promise you that. I'll be looking for an epidural too.

• • •

ROSIE helps APRIL to sit back on the side of the bed.

ROSIE: Brown...

APRIL: Green...

ROSIE: Larry Keenan hasn't...

APRIL: Clarke Gable has.

• • •

SEAN helps ANNA onto the side of the bed so that she is back to back with APRIL.

ANNA: I've been so scared, frightened to take anything for granted... just praying to God the child may be born safe...

• • •

ROSIE: I promise you'll stand here with your first born.

• • •

SEAN: (*Kneeling to take off ANNA's shoes*) I promise you it will.

• • •

APRIL: And will you be the Godmother?

ROSIE: I'll carry her up to Corpus Christi for you wrapped in that shawl from Mammy's wardrobe.

● ● ●

SEAN: And we'll bring him home here together, the pair of us frightened out of our wits, as if he were about to explode.

SEAN stands back so that his pose echoes that of ROSIE on the far side of the bed.

● ● ●

ROSIE: (*Making the sign of the cross*) I baptise you in the name of the Father and the Son...

APRIL: It's unlucky.

ROSIE: Patricia Jonathan Keenan Clarke Bright Gable.

APRIL: And we'll bring him back here?

ROSIE: We'll bring them all back here.

● ● ●

SEAN: And the first thing we'll do is carry him...

ANNA: Or her...

SEAN: Up here to show him his room.

● ● ●

APRIL: Look baby, see how bright the world is out there.

● ● ●

SEAN: With all the trees coming into bloom by the college.

ANNA: (*Unconsciously lifting her hands*) And I'll hold her in my arms here.

● ● ●

APRIL: How tiny and precious you are in my arms.

● ● ●

ANNA: Of course she won't actually be able to see...

● ● ●

APRIL: Just how enormous everything will be.

● ● ●

ANNA: Just how beautiful the world is going to look. You know, I'm so frightened and yet I can't wait...

● ● ●

APRIL: Just to hold you in my arms.

● ● ●

ANNA: Baby Bunting, how beautiful tomorrow is going to look for you.

● ● ●

APRIL: And all the beautiful tomorrows to come.

● ● ●

ANNA: Wobbly legs learning to walk across in that park.

• • •

APRIL: Little legs learning to walk.

• • •

ANNA: And all the happiness that you will bring...

• • •

APRIL: All the happiness that I shall know...

• • •

ANNA: When I hold you up here...

• • •

APRIL: When I hold you up in the light...

• • •

ANNA: My bright shiny new penny...

• • •

APRIL: My sweet, sweet child...

• • •

ANNA: Our precious child to come.

The End

BLINDED BY THE LIGHT

A comedy in two acts

"*Blinded by the Light* can properly be described as hysterically funny, its wild humour being always on the edge of dementia. It is in many ways a parable of Ireland's referenda years, the years in which the notion of private conscience became impossible, the years of the undermining of that wonderful right defined by the American Supreme Court as "the right to be left alone". The play's hero, Mick, is a Dublin Canute, trying to staunch the flow of the sea as it pours across the threshold of his bed-sit in the form of the Mormons, the Legion of Mary, interfering landlords and would-be friends. The comedy is freewheeling, absurd, associative, handled with immense skill and wit by an author whose taste in bad taste is impeccable. It zig-zags between theatre of the absurb and kitchen comedy, between farce and social realism in ways that are always highly entertaining."
— *Irish Times*

"A classic piece of Irish comedy. Unless you're dead from the neck up you'll love it." — *The Arts Show, RTE*

"Manically madcap and hilariously funny, Dermot Bolger's play *Blinded by the Light* canters in a bawdy romp onto the stage, hearding the arrival of a unique comic writing talent. Energentic, perfectly timed and brilliantly observed, *Blinded by the Light* works and is a very, very funny play not to be missed. — *Irish Press*

"Great fun and outrageously funny. Dermot Bolger has a mighty comic talent." — *Evening Press*

"A circus of sex, drugs, religions, drink and a saint... with the essential impetus for farce — the release and control of madness, all just sitting atop truth. Excellent." — *The Cork Examiner*

Blinded by the Light was first produced by the Abbey Theatre Dublin, on its Peacock stage, on the 6th of March, 1990.

Directed by	Caroline FitzGerald

Cast:

Mick	Donal O'Kelly
Siobhan	Alison Deegan
Scottish Gentleman	Wesley Murphy
Shay	Eamonn Hunt
Bosco	Frank Kelly
Ollie	Gerard Byrne
Pascal	Phelim Drew
Elder Stanford	Enda Oates
Elder Osborne	Michael James Ford
Lily	Máire Ní Ghráinne
Jack	Maurie Taylor
Mr Lewis	Kevin Flood
Sean	Owen Roe

Designer	Chisato Yoshimi
Lighting/Production Manager	Trevor Dawson
Stage Manager	John Kells
Stage Director	John Stapleton
Assistant Stage Manager	Fearga O'Doherty
Sound	Dave Nolan

The play is set in a Dublin bed-sit. Apart from Joe Dolan, the choice of all other music is optional and may be updated.

The author would like to express his thanks to everyone involved in this first production, especially its director, Caroline FitzGerald.

For George, naturally

ACT ONE

Scene One

In blackout we hear Joe Dolan finish singing 'Make Me an Island'. The song dies, followed by momentary static after which seemingly from below the stage, Joe Dolan starts to sing 'The House with the Whitewashed Gables'. The stage is in darkness through which we can discern the outline of MICK's untidy bed-sit, crammed with stolen hardbacked library books. The top half of the back wall may be in the form of a gauze, which appears solid when the bed-sit is ordinarily lit, but transparent when the bed-sit is in darkness and the hallway (running behind it) is lit. However this corridor can also be left totally unseen if director and designer see fit.

We hear a door open and the soft click of a light switch in the hall, so that a low arc of light appears beneath the doorway of the bed-sit from the corridor behind it, or else the gauze is lit up so that we can see the outline of figures approach. There is the clatter of footsteps, the clink of bottles and the drunken murmur of OLLIE, PASCAL and BOSCO in the corridor, all of whom have heavy Drogheda accents.

OLLIE: Jaysus, I'm a tad sick of Joe Dolan! Who's the header downstairs always playing him?

PASCAL: Lord knows. He never goes out. That oul acid's a bad man.

There is the sudden explosion of glass as bottles are dropped and smash on the floor.

PASCAL: Buck it, Bosco can you not hold your drink at your age?

BOSCO: Not in them plastic bags from the off-licence. They make them fierce thin. You'd miss the oul brown ones.

OLLIE: We'll be a tad short of drink tonight.

There is a jangling noise as BOSCO searches for his keys. The front door opens again with a thunderous noise.

SHAY: (*In a voice filled with irritation*) Jaysus, not Joe Dolan! I'll blast that spacer out of it! (*He strides up the corridor, holding a tall object*) Is he in yet? (*SHAY hammers on the bed-sit door*) Where is he at all? Does he not know he'll have to be up for work in the morning? (*Pause*) Well, shag him anyway, yous can have this so. Do yous want it?

PASCAL: Never get that bucking thing on the provincial bus.

SHAY: (*Annoyed*) What's wrong with it? Solid bleeding steel, fierce useful too. Ah, suit yourselves. I'll show this bastard downstairs.

We hear SHAY stomp upstairs as a key is turned and the other characters exit into BOSCO's room, the unseen door of which would be directly opposite MICK's. As BOSCO's door closes and the corridor light switches itself off we hear Lou Reed's 'Walk on the Wild Side' being switched on loudly by SHAY upstairs, the choruses of both songs merging. The front door opens, quieter now and the hall light comes on again. SIOBHAN laughs in the corridor.

MICK: (*Low, drunken voice*) Say nothing to nobody in this madhouse, just follow me.

SIOBHAN: (*Incredulous laugh*) You keep it indoors?

MICK: Sure, you'd have to. It's a vintage model. One speck of rust could knock its value in half.

The bed-sit door opens and MICK and SIOBHAN not so much walk as stumble into the room which is now lit by a shaft of light from the corridor. Neither is too sober. There is just enough light to make out their movements.

MICK: Caution is required. Hands and knees only from here on.

He sinks to his knees, clinking the bottle in his pocket, and with another incredulous giggle SIOBHAN joins him and follows MICK who crawls across the worn carpet towards a bedside locker. He stops so that she almost knocks into him. MICK opens a drawer and removes something so small that the audience cannot see what it is. He places it on the floor and points towards it as SIOBHAN peers down.

SIOBHAN: I've walked a mile and a half to see that?

MICK: It was worth it, wasn't it?

SIOBHAN: (*Quoting him*) "Vintage model. Family heirloom."

MICK: You asked if I had a car. Sure didn't God give you legs. What do you want a car for?

SIOBHAN kneels up, swaying slightly, to look at him.

SIOBHAN: You were going to give me a ride in in.

MICK: I don't remember anything about "in it."

SIOBHAN: (*Darkly*) Well, a lift home then.

MICK kneels up as well, the jokiness gone from his voice.

MICK: (*Softly*) You don't really want to go home, do you?

There is silence between them for a second.

SIOBHAN: (*Softly*) Well, maybe not just...

The room is suddenly flooded with light by SHAY who stands in the doorway, holding an uprooted bus-stop pole in one hand. We see the bed-sit properly for the first time. The top of

*the wardrobe had a pyramid of empty Ovaltine tins, while a
number of golf clubs lean against one wall and a guitar
slumbers in one corner with four strings. The only armchair
is inhabited by a family of quite grotesque soft toys. Over the
single bed an ITGWU "Strike On Here" picket has been hung
up and underneath it there is a poster of the Irish Soccer team
framed by a green-and-white scarf. To the stage right of the
bed there is a locker and to the stage left of the bed a chest of
drawers has been constructed against the back wall. This
chest of drawers is actually a hollow cavity which opens out
onto the back stage area, with a secret sliding panel on top.
There is an opening in the wall, stage left, hung with plastic
strips as if leading into a shower unit and a curtained window
in the wall beside it. In the other wall, stage right, there is an
old fashioned fire-place, constructed so as to give the illusion
of flames when a fire is lit. There is also a small table and a
battered sofa. Books run in a long row on the floor along the
walls on all side, yet the bed-sit is neatly kept in a haphazard
way.*

SHAY: (*Ignoring SIOBHAN who kneels startled*) Where have
you been till now? Don't you know you've got to be up for
work in the morning? You needn't think I'm phoning in for
you again. (*Slightest pause*) So, do you want a bus stop or
not?

MICK: (*Rising in restrained annoyance*) Shay...

SHAY: Solid steel. Where would you get the like?

*MICK removes a long overcoat from the coat stand beside his
bed to reveal that the stand is made from a bus stop.*

MICK: ... you already gave me one.

SHAY: Can't you take the two and breed them? You're never
bleeding happy.

*As SHAY talks, BOSCO, PASCAL and OLLIE crowd through
the door behind him.*

BOSCO: What? A poker session is it? Great stuff.

BOSCO grabs the deck of cards on the table and begins to shuffle them. OLLIE kneels beside the stereo and begins to pull CDs out all over the floor while PASCAL wanders past SIOBHAN to root for food in the presses above the sink.

PASCAL: (*Nodding to SIOBHAN*) How's it goin'. Bucking bad dose of the munchies.

He finds a packet of digestive biscuits and starts to wolf them.

SHAY: (*Referring to BOSCO as he lets the bus stop rest against the wall*) Don't let him deal. We'll be here all night.

SHAY pulls up a chair.

BOSCO: (*Protesting*) Ah now, house rules, dealers choice.

MICK: Lads! (*Louder*) Lads!

They stop and look at him.

SHAY: Alright, Bosco can deal, but play something we can open with. Any of them mushrooms left from last night, Mick? It's no wonder them old monks were mad bastards seeing visions. (*He looks at MICK who's trying to communicate with him*) What?

MICK indicates SIOBHAN.

SHAY: Oh yeah. (*He does a quick headcount*) No, it's okay, we can deal with six off the one deck. Just reshuffle the shite.

MICK: (*Abandoning hope in sign language*) Out lads!

SHAY: (*Catching on*) Oh yeah. Right.

He picks up the bus stop as he exits, followed by OLLIE with loose CDs under his arm and PASCAL still clutching the biscuits. When they're gone BOSCO looks up.

BOSCO: A round of In-Betweenies to deal?

He looks around at the empty bed-sit in surprise.

MICK: (*Firmly*) Good night Bosco.

BOSCO exits, finally catching on. MICK closes the door, then looks at SIOBHAN. The jokey intimacy between them is broken.

SIOBHAN: Expecting anyone else before I go?

MICK: What's your hurry?

SIOBHAN: Listen, it's late... sure, I'll see you again some time.

MICK: (*Appealing with a half-shrug*) Okay, so I don't own a car.

SIOBHAN: (*Smiles*) I never cared if you did. You were on my way home.

MICK: (*Glancing at the floor*) It's a pretty classy dinky, mind you. It shows character.

SIOBHAN: (*Laughs*) It shows neck. (*Uncertain pause*) I better go... it's late.

MICK: (*Producing a bottle of brandy from his pocket*) Go on, have one drink anyway... before you go.

SIOBHAN takes a slug and hands it back to him, as she rises to her feet. MICK stares at her as she brushes her clothes down, then scans the ceiling wistfully. SIOBHAN looks at him.

SIOBHAN: Are you alright?

MICK: Ah yeah. I was just... thinking.

SIOBHAN: What?

MICK: If pigs could fly.

SIOBHAN: (*Puzzled*) What?

MICK: (*Tentatively, with an impish grin*) You wouldn't *really* want to go home.

SIOBHAN scans the ceiling as well as if studiously examining something.

SIOBHAN: Well... maybe I don't (*pause*) just yet. Back seats bore me anyway.

MICK: This one has a special feature.

He lifts the dinky car up and hands it to her, pointing to the driver's door. SIOBHAN opens it and prises something out with her finger. She holds up a small plastic bag.

MICK: Of course it's a small model, but I've taken some nice trips in in.

SIOBHAN: The last of the famous mushrooms.

MICK: (*Pointing at a battered television, balanced precariously on a mound of books*) The only way to get colour on that set. Try some.

SIOBHAN looks around the flat, then up at the bare light bulb.

SIOBHAN: (*Suggestively*) They'd taste nicer after dark.

MICK grins and hands her the brandy. SIOBHAN swallows a couple of stringy mushrooms as MICK switches off the light, plunging the stage into darkness. We hear him staggering slightly as he begins to grope around the bed-sit for her.

MICK: Siobhan? (*More worried*) Siobhan? Ah now don't go asleep on me. Sio...

He gives a startled shout as SIOBHAN suddenly lunges onto his back.

SIOBHAN: (*Mock Oriental accent*) Kato!

MICK: Good Jaysus, ahhh...

There is the creak of springs as they land on the bed.

MICK: Never spilt a drop. My God, you're a woman with class.

SIOBHAN: Have you glasses?

MICK: Why, have you germs?

There is the noise of drinking.

SIOBHAN: (*Giggles*) Wait, you're spilling it on me.

MICK: Don't worry, I'll lick it off.

We hear the rustle of clothes and sounds of heavy breathing as 'Caption Beaky' begins to play in BOSCO's flat, adding to the chorus of background noise.

SIOBHAN: The music, can you not kill the music?

There is a click as MICK turns on the bed-sit lamp. SIOBHAN and himself are beneath the sheets.

MICK: No, but I can drown it.

He climbs out of bed in his underpants, flicks on his stereo, turns off the light again and dives back into bed as the stage is filled with the swelling chorus of 'They Got Elvis on a UFO' as if sung by strangulated ducks on speed while MICK and SIOBHAN moan.

Scene Two

Night gives way to morning as lights rise to suggest the sun battling through the pulled curtains. A bird twitters outside the window. The empty brandy bottle lies on the floor near the bed. MICK gradually raises his head as though it were a painful and delicate operation. A look of shock crosses his face when he discovers the body beside him. His head sinks

*back onto the pillow. The movement wakes SIOBHAN who
tries to focus her eyes on the unfamiliar room, then sits up
with a jerk and stares down at MICK before her head also
sinks back. After a moment she cuddles against him.*

SIOBHAN: (*Affectionate but slightly awkward, unsure of
what response she will receive*) Am I still your cuddly toy?
(*MICK groans faintly*) Is my voice still sweeter than Christy
O'Connor Jr playing the spoons?

MICK: (*Weakly*) Oh God.

SIOBHAN: Still you were great all the same, Lance.

MICK: My name's Mick. I told you I had a lance.

SIOBHAN: Only teasing. (*More seriously*) Listen Mick, I'll
be late for work. Have you any food in the gaff? (*MICK moans
piteously*) What's wrong?

MICK: My life's passing before my eyes. I hate repeats.

SIOBHAN: Food. What do you have for breakfast?

MICK: (*Sighs*) A cigarette, a shite and a good look around.

SIOBHAN: Be serious.

MICK: (*Pulling himself together*) Sorry, I generally dine out.
I'm a bit disorganised.

SIOBHAN: (*looking around*) And the seven dwarfs were a bit
short. Here, I've got to go to work.

*She begins putting on items of underclothing in bed, then
wiggles out to quickly get into her dress. It is very obviously
a fairly daring night-time outfit.*

MICK: In that?

SIOBHAN: (*Smiles*) I had only gone out for a pint of milk.

MICK: Those are the dangerous times.

*There is an awkward silence with neither knowing what to
say.*

MICK: (*Tentatively*) Siobhan?

SIOBHAN: (*Hopefully*) Yes Mick.

MICK: Could I ask you a very great favour?

SIOBHAN: (*Pause*) You know you don't have to.

MICK: No... I want to.

SIOBHAN: (*Coyly*) Ask away then.

MICK: You wouldn't phone in sick for me?

SIOBHAN's disappointment is visible, but she says nothing.

MICK: The mobile libraries. The number's on the wall beside the hall phone.

SIOBHAN: What will I tell them?

MICK: (*Thinks*) Playschool's on television.

SIOBHAN: You enjoy Playschool?

MICK: (*Sighs*) It certainly beats work.

SIOBHAN: I've got to tell them something.

MICK tries to think of an excuse but too many brain cells have been lost in the night.

MICK: (*Weakly*) You could tell them I've taken to the bed.

SIOBHAN: (*Sighs*) Leave it to me. Michael...?

MICK: Flaherty. Miss Siobhan...?

SIOBHAN: (*Indignant*) Mrs! (*Smiles*) Ms Connolly.

She exits, leaving the flat door open. MICK holds his head carefully in both hands. We hear her dialling and her indistinct voice phoning in sick for him. There is the sound of heavy footsteps in the hall and of a door opening.

SHAY: (*Offstage, with a laugh*) Morning Bosco! Any more of the Drogheda boat people arrive in the meantime?.

BOSCO: (*Offstage*) That's not funny you know. (*Quieter, in reply to muffled sounds behind him*) What? He said nothing lads, never mind him.

SHAY enters MICK's bed-sit indignantly, holding an envelope in his outstretched hand. He walks straight across the bed to glance through the curtains suspiciously, as MICK looks up wearily at him.

SHAY: Is she gone? I hope you scored better than I did at the poker. (*He turns to thrust the letter at MICK in the bed*) Okay, so tell me I'm imagining it this time. What's that?

He points towards the back of the envelope. MICK takes it from him as SHAY returns to the window to suspiciously survey the street outside.

MICK: Ever learn to knock, Shay? (*He examines the envelope*) It's a quarter-inch gap where your dear mother ran out of lip. What's it doing outside?

SHAY: (*Turning*) Pissing rain. It's been opened. It's obvious. A fool could see it. Any mushrooms left?

MICK: (*Handing the letter back to him*) My granny. Listen Shay, I don't know how to break this to you.

SHAY: (*Worried*) What? Have you seen someone? I *knew* your man wasn't sheltering from the rain at that bus stop across the road last week.

MICK: (*Slowly as if a foreigner with little English*) Nobody is opening your mail. Nobody is tapping the telephone. Nobody is watching the house. The great wide world out there doesn't know who you are and it doesn't give a shite.

SHAY: (*Snatching the letter back indignantly*) You just watch who you're calling a nonentity, right!

SHAY storms out, meeting SIOBHAN on her way in.

SHAY: (*Looking at SIOBHAN's outfit*) Come on, ye divil, ye!

SIOBHAN: (*Coldly*) Go on yourself. Slap it up on the table and we'll see what you're made of. (*She turns to MICK as SHAY exits*) Who's your friend?

MICK: The Mata Hari of Mountmellick.

SIOBHAN: I believe you. (*Briskly, reaching for her coat*) It's a bit of a waste, isn't it?

MICK: What?

SIOBHAN: Having doors around here. Anyway, you're in business.

MICK: (*Snuggling down in the bed*) Thanks.

SIOBHAN: How do you feel?

MICK: Like the song said, My head hurts, my feet stink and I don't love Jesus.

SIOBHAN: (*Turning to leave*) I doubt if you love anything.

MICK: That's not fair. I love St Martin, Patron Saint of Hopeless Causes.

SIOBHAN: St Jude is hopeless causes.

MICK: All foreign bodies look the same to me. Anyway, you wouldn't want to rely on the living when you follow Shelbourne Football Club.

SIOBHAN: (*Pausing at the door in surprise*) Shelbourne? Good God, you are a romantic. Ben Hannigan?

MICK: (*Lifting himself up on one elbow in surprise*) Ben Hannigan?

SIOBHAN: Eric Barber. Paddy Roche. (*Deliberately fumbles, then drops her bag.*) The safest pair of hands since the Venus de Milo!

MICK: (*Stunned*) You weren't even born when he played.

SIOBHAN: It was half-price admisssion for embryos. I almost didn't come out when I smelt the watery Bovril.

MICK: The smell of my childhood, Tolka Park. Surely I must have seen you there?

SIOBHAN: My Da used to take me to the terraces. They reminded him of his country childhood, acres of open spaces where you'd never meet a soul.

MICK: My God, you were that blob at the far end of the ground. I always thought it was a seagull with a broken wing.

SIOBHAN: My brothers used to bar me from the twenty-questions sessions. I had to bribe my way back in with cigarettes.

MICK: (*Thinks*) Who played eleven minutes on his debut for Ireland and scored an equaliser away from home?

SIOBHAN: Joe Waters of course. Turkey.

MICK: Are you a vision or real?

SIOBHAN: What's the smallest country ever to field a team in a European club championship match?

MICK: What? Wait.. (*He lifts the blankets and looks down*) I'm not dressed, it's not fair. (*He thinks*) Andorra?

SIOBHAN: Litchenstein.

MICK: (*Winces*) Don't mention Litchenstein! I'd bar you from my shed as well. (*Pause*) Siobhan?

SIOBHAN: What?

MICK: Can I ask you a really, really great favour?

SIOBHAN: I don't make breakfast.

MICK: No, seriously. Listen I'm no good at this sort of thing. You're not seeing me at my best here. I've wanted to ask you since I woke up, but I just... well, couldn't get a way around to it. (*Pause*) Can I see you again?

SIOBHAN: You don't have to.

MICK: I want to.

SIOBHAN: Maybe.

MICK: Please. Pretty please.

SIOBHAN: (*Smiles*) Okay.

MICK: Tomorrow night?

SIOBHAN: Tomorrow night.

MICK: George's Street?

SIOBHAN: Where?

MICK: The glass shelter at the 16 bus stop.

SIOBHAN: Why? Where are we going?

MICK: Harold's Cross dog track, of course. I mean it is a Thursday.

SIOBHAN: Don't wait after midnight if I'm not there.

MICK: If you don't come I promise to throw myself in front of the mechanical hare. It will be on your conscience that I was savaged by muzzled greyhounds!

MICK grins and she blows him a kiss as she is about to close the door. Behind her there is a sudden evacuation of bodies from BOSCO's flat.

BOSCO: (*Offstage*) Cheers lads.

SIOBHAN is forced back into the room followed by PASCAL.

PASCAL: (*To SIOBHAN*) Still here? Well, how did yous make out together, so?

OLLIE: (*Offstage*) See you next week, Bosco.

OLLIE appears in the doorway ready to pull PASCAL back out into the corridor.

OLLIE: Will you come on, Pascal. You'll be interrupting all class of tears and recriminations. (*He looks towards the window*) That's not rain, is it? It's a tad wet. Sure, will we go home at all?

BOSCO: (*Anxiously, offstage*) Ah now, it's only a shower, lads.

PASCAL: (*Staring at the window*) Ah, buck it...bucking oul rain bucking down.

SIOBHAN stares at PASCAL mumbling to himself, almost in a world of his own.

OLLIE: Ah don't mind him Miss, a tad inarticulate in the mornings.

PASCAL: (*Glaring at OLLIE*) Buck off you, I am not. I never bucking wet the bucking bed yet.

SIOBHAN steps back as the two lads vanish down the hall. The front door slams and she looks at MICK.

SIOBHAN: (*Unsure if she heard right*) Bucking?

MICK: Pascal's Ma made him swear on Saint Oliver Plunkett's head that a curse would never pass his lips.

SIOBHAN: Get away.

MICK: That's the Dublin branch of the Drogheda United Supporters Club next door.

SIOBHAN: (*Sneaking a glance across*) No wonder the room's so small.

She goes to exit again.

MICK: One last thing.

SIOBHAN: (*Stops*) What?

MICK: Eh, you wouldn't just fill the kettle while you're there?

SIOBHAN: How do you get to be so lazy?

MICK: Hard work and practice.

She quickly fills the kettle beside her, switches it on and heads for the door.

SIOBHAN: Goodbye, Mick.

SIOBHAN exits, closing the door. MICK waits a moment then throws his fist in the air in celebration before suddenly grimacing and holding his head again.

MICK: Love. It must be love. (*He thinks, then shouts after her*) Siobhan? Do you play snooker? (*No reply. He talks to himself quietly*) There must be a catch: her mother's a Fianna Fail Councillor, her father sleeps with the Bishop of Clonfert. Nobody can be that nice. (*He raises a hand to his head*) Gentle does it. Lie there and relax. Dangerous to get up too quickly on a Wednesday.

He lies back, then rises on one elbow to reach for his trousers on the floor. He raids each pocket and loose change rains from them until, from the pile of coins on the bed, he picks up and unfurls a crumpled five pound note.

MICK: A note? On a Wednesday? A beggar must have given it to me.

He continues searching his pockets and finally an equally crumpled packet of cigarettes is discovered. He lights one and is lost in a violent fit of coughing.

MICK: That's better. (*Pause*) Litchenstein?

He searches the bedclothes and discovers a small piece of silver foil.

MICK: Thanks be to God for lust. There's still some dope left.

He rises on one elbow to reach for a sweeping brush under the bed. He uses it to knock over a small pile of books on the floor and sweeps four hardbacked volumes across the floor towards him. He bends down to pick them up.

MICK: (*Examining the books*) Who have we got this morning? Ceaser's *Gallic Wars* in Latin; Arthur Schopenhauer, he's the boy to put manners on you during a peaceful morning in bed; *Winnie the Pooh*, we could live with that; Churchill's *History of the Second World War, Volume Six* — Jaysus, if that one wasn't stolen I'd bring it back. No, definitely Schopenhauer, there's too much sex and violence in the others for a Wednesday. (*Mock radio presenter's voice*) But first, a word from our sponsors.

MICK briefly looks up, hearing footsteps in the hall and a knocking on BOSCO's door, as he opens the packet of cigarette papers, sticks two together on top of the book, breaks open a cigarette and empties half the tobacco onto the skins before opening the silver foil. He begins to crumple the hash carefully over the tobacco, then searches his pockets and looks around.

MICK: Roach paper. Never any shagging roach paper. (*He looks at the books*) Shag this intellectual snobbery, will I never remember to steal some softbacks in work for a change?

There are three sudden knocks on the own door. He looks round in alarm, carefully picks up the book with the half rolled joint on it, rises from the bed reluctantly and is about to put it under the bed when, simultaneously, the knocking reoccurs and he is seized by another fit of coughing which scatters the contents of the cigarette papers over the floor.

MICK: Alright, I'm coming.

He gets into his jeans and opens the door cautiously.

ELDER OSBORNE: (*Offstage in a strong American accent*) Very sorry to trouble you Sir. We're just doing a survey and we were wondering if you would mind answering a few questions?

MICK: (*Stepping back slightly so that we can see ELDER OSBORNE and ELDER STANFORD*) Eh... no offence like but I'm very busy just now...

ELDER OSBORNE: It won't take a moment.

MICK: And I'm skint.

ELDER OSBORNE: (*Hurt voice*) We're not salesmen.

MICK: (*Peering at them again*) Oh, sorry. Jehovah Witnesses?

ELDER OSBORNE: (*Even more offended*) We are from the Church of Latter Day Saints of Jesus Christ! (*MICK looks blank*) Mormons.

MICK: I know how you feel lads, somebody called me a Bohs fan once. Actually I'm not really religious. So nothing personal, but...

ELDER OSBORNE: Oh good! You're the very person we want to talk to so.

MICK: I am? (*Pause*) How did you get in, boys?

ELDER STANFORD: The front door was open to receive us.

MICK: I'll strangle that Bosco. Listen, I've a very sore head, lads.

ELDER OSBORNE: Well the fact is Mr...?

MICK: Mick.

ELDER OSBORNE: The fact is Michael that we could have finished the survey in the time we've been discussing this.

MICK: How many doors have you knocked on this morning?

ELDER OSBORNE: Nobody ever said the work of the Lord was easy. "In the desert prepare / The way for the Lord / Make straight in the wilderness / A highway for the Lord." Isaiah 40:3.

MICK: "Anyone who's been turned down / Is bound to be a friend of mine. " John Prine. And I suppose it is raining. I haven't the strength to argue. Five minutes though to get dry and that's it.

He steps back and the two MORMONS eagerly enter the bed-sit. They are young, perfectly dressed with glasses and very sincere. ELDER OSBORNE is the more senior of them and inclined to take the lead. ELDER STANFORD is inclined to follow the text book in everything but increasingly as the play progresses he begins to overstep the mark, annoying ELDER OSBORNE. They survey the room with a look of vague disbelief. The kettle is boiling and MICK goes over to it. He selects the least dirty cup, tosses in a tea bag and fills it up. In this scene MICK is as much amused as bewildered by his visitors.

MICK: Eh tea? (*ELDER OSBORNE coughs and they both shake their heads.*) Sorry. Eh... coffee? Jaysus that's worse.

ELDER OSBORNE: Hot water. Thank you.

MICK: Oh yeah.

He rinses two more cups, fills them with hot water and brings them over to the two chairs when THE MORMONS have sat down. They smile, take them off him and each have a sip.

MICK: (*At a loss*) Eh... is it strong enough?

Both smile and nod. MICK sits on the edge of the bed with his tea. There is silence as the visitors look around.

ELDER OSBORNE: Nice place.

MICK: Thanks.

ELDER STANFORD: God groweth even in the wilderness.

ELDER STANFORD smiles across at his companion. Having gained entry, they now seem content to sit in silence.

MICK: (*Cautiously*) It was just a couple of questions wasn't it? (*They smile in reply*) Do you... eh... think you could ask them?

ELDER STANFORD: We will.

Yet they continue looking around them.

MICK: (*Hopefully*) Soon?

ELDER STANFORD: In time.

ELDER OSBORNE: Often when people turn us away I think it is not to us they are refusing to open their doors but to themselves, not us they are afraid of but their own souls. Are you frightened of us, Michael, or of your spiritual self?

MICK: Religion's a dangerous business lads. Why not just take the weight off your feet and enjoy the hot water?

ELDER OSBORNE: What possible harm could it do you?

MICK: Look at Cyril Knowles' brother. Gave up playing for Wolves that season they could have won the Cup.

ELDER OSBORNE: Flippancy is the weapon those who are hurt always hide behind. You were not busy this morning when we called, Michael. (*He nods towards the bed*) You were still lying there.

MICK: It's only half-nine boys.

ELDER STANFORD: (*Butts in*) This is what they call "the front line" in training. Fine able-bodied creatures like you cast off on the scrap heap of society, itching to work if you could only find a job.

MICK starts to grin, amused at the conversation.

ELDER OSBORNE: I feel for you Michael in your helplessness. (*He leans forward*) What were your thoughts this morning as you rose from your lonely bed?

MICK: Well eh... (*Mumbles*) it was a bit crowded actually.

ELDER OSBORNE: Could you have known friends were so close at hand? That Elder Stanford and I were walking these streets at that very moment?

ELDER STANFORD: (*Leaning forward also*) Knocking on doors, searching for the right one. It is the black sheep the good shepherd will look for. Is that right, Elder Osborne?

MICK: (*At a loss*) I was never much into sheep meself. Saw this film once in Holland, but... eh... never mind.

ELDER STANFORD: You were crying in the wilderness, thinking no one could hear and yet He hears everything. We have found you in time to lift you from this squalor, this degradation...

MICK: Ah hold on now. I was going to clean it up.

ELDER STANFORD: ...to lead you back to the light of God.

MICK: I don't want to be rude boys, but you're barking up the wrong tree.

ELDER OSBORNE: Doubts are natural. We will answer all your questions in time.

MICK: Is this all in the questionnaire?

ELDER OSBORNE: We don't need a questionnaire, Michael, to see the way you are, to feel your despair without a job or a future, with nobody to share your burden. Michael, we have come to share the burden. To tell you it is not your fault. We know how you are suppressed with your socialist newspapers and your left-wing governments, your communist health service and newscasters taking their orders from Moscow. And you are their helpless victim, forced out of work by their unemployment incentive, stripped of your freedom by their rent allowances.

MICK: Merciful hour. The magic mushrooms weren't in it.

ELDER OSBORNE: We know your shame, but we have come here to talk of joy, to lead you out into the light. Michael, I want to leave you this book. I know you have a thousand questions to ask, a thousand barriers to break down that you have built around your true self. Those questions will all be answered in time. (*He reaches into his briefcase.*) Read this book for now.

MICK: Whatever you're on it's great stuff lads, but your five minutes is up. (*ELDER OSBORNE produces a hardback volume which he holds out to MICK*) Listen lads, I've just got this aversion to joining anything and I've a lot of reading of my own to get through. No disrespect but... (*A new note enters his voice as he looks at the book*) eh... you don't have one with a cardboard cover, do you?

THE MORMONS smile at each other.

ELDER STANFORD: Humility is the first sign of repentance.

ELDER OSBORNE: Take this one, Michael. You deserve the best.

MICK: (*Humbly*) No, I couldn't.

He hands it back to ELDER STANFORD who produces a softbound edition which he places in MICK's hands.

ELDER OSBORNE: I am touched, Michael, by your humility.

MICK: (*Raising a hand modestly*) No, say nothing. Please. But if you don't mind, I... eh.. have some thinking to do.

ELDER OSBORNE: Of course, Michael. Good bye for now. (*to ELDER STANFORD*) A sign, Elder Stanford, after all our walking.

MICK shows them to the door, shakes their hands and closes the door after them. He lies against it in relief, then looks down at the book in his hand, examines the cover carefully before tearing a small strip off it. He rolls the cardboard expertly between his fingers, then looks up.

MICK: (*Delighted*) Bleeding great roach paper!

Suddenly below him 'Paper Roses' sung by Maisie McDaniel, starts to play in the basement flat. He looks down and frowns as the stage goes dark.

Scene Three

The music fades. The lights go up again, lit for evening. The bed-sit looks the same, except that the book MICK was given is displayed on the bedside locker, with most of its front cover gone. MICK enters, leaving the door open and after a quick look through the curtains, exits again to return with two auctioneers' signs, one large and the other small. He throws them down near the fireplace into which he throws a half-packet of firelighters and, taking up an axe, begins to chop up the smaller sign and pile the pieces into the grate. There is a knocking on the closed door and MICK looks around in panic as if searching for a way out.

MICK: (*Quietly, looking towards heaven*) Not again, Lord. (*Louder*) Who is it?

BOSCO: (*offstage*) Are those bastards from Drogheda around, Mick? Is it safe?

MICK looks visibly relieved as he opens the door. Although dressed in scruffy jeans and a dirty tee-shirt BOSCO is actually almost forty years of age. He has a look of perpetual adolescence and the pallor of objects rarely exposed to daylight. He enters with both hands locked together as if in prayer and his eyes fixed on the small hole formed by the thumb of his left hand and index finger of his right.

MICK: The wetbacks hasn't arrived tonight. They must have stepped up petrols on the Louth border.

BOSCO: The shaggers have my life destroyed. Even the provincial bus driver is starting to stop outside the front door. Ever since Ollie's Da died and he inherited the disability pass.

MICK: You know your bed-sit isn't exactly Venice in springtime.

BOSCO: Beats shagging Drogheda on the dole. Oh, I can't blame the lads. You get up in the morning, walk down the town, into the cathedral for a gawk at Oliver Plunkett's head, home for dinner, back down, another gander at the head, walk round in the pissings of rain, back in for a last look at the head. All there has been to do in Drogheda for the last three hundred years is look at the head of Saint Oliver Plunkett.

MICK has resumed chopping up the sign at the fireplace.

MICK: When are they due?

BOSCO: Today or tomorrow. They've got to get the dole for their brothers who are over in Boston on the black.

MICK: Why can't they collect it in Drogheda?

BOSCO: Sure they've to collect it for themselves up there.

MICK notices BOSCO's hands and nods towards them.

MICK: Wanker's cramp, is it?

BOSCO: (*Looking down and remembering*) Oh yeah. Any Blu-Tack Mick?

MICK: Somewhere.

BOSCO: Find it quick, my hands are killing me.

MICK removes a poster from the wall and rolls up the four bits of Blu-Tack from the back of it.

BOSCO: Stick it in there, go on.

MICK presses the Blu-Tack into the valley between BOSCO's hands and when it is wedged there BOSCO finally releases them and stares at the lump of Blu-Tack in his palm.

BOSCO: You're a mate. Com'ere, (*He looks around*) is it cool to roll?

MICK: Yeah, sure.

BOSCO: Oh great. (*Stops and thinks.*) Have you any dope?

MICK: (*Sighs*) In my jacket pocket.

BOSCO: Fair play to you. (*He goes to pick up MICK's jacket, then stops to show MICK the Blu-Tack*) So, what ya think?

MICK: Very nice Blu-Tack. Good vintage I'm sure.

BOSCO: No, the size of it? (*MICK still has no idea what the conversation is about.*) For thirty spots, what do ya think?

MICK: What are you on about, Bosco?

BOSCO: I met this mot in a pub, and she offered it to me. Won't have it till Friday but it's a thirty-spot deal. Moroccan Black. I made a hole in my hands (*He joins them together again*) and I said to her is it that size, or this size and she said it was this size. (*He holds up the Blu-Tack*) So what you think? Thirty spots? Did I do well?

MICK: You paid her cash?

There is a sudden knocking on the door and BOSCO throws the Blu-Tack away from him onto the chair.

BOSCO: (*Alarmed*) The Drug Squad! How they find out so fast?

MICK: You're okay, Blu-Tack isn't prescribed yet. (*Calls politely*) Who is it?

ELDER OSBORNE: (*Offstage*) Glad we caught you in again, Michael.

MICK: Why me Lord? Why me?

Quickly MICK opens the locker and takes out empty bottles of spirits and wine to pile up on the table. He grabs the jar of coffee and the tea bags to display prominently, lights three cigarettes, puts one of them smoking away in the ash tray, one between his lips and the third in BOSCO's surprised mouth.

BOSCO: Oh cheers, you're a mate. What is it, another poker session? I'm skint after that one last night. We didn't get out of here until dawn.

MICK: Only two rules for a life of contemplation and retreat, Bosco. Never leave the bed on a Wednesday unless you really have to and never ever run short of roach paper.

MICK is about to answer the knock when he spies the book with the cover almost gone. He puts it under the mattress, then opens the door.

MICK: (*Wearily*) The third time this week, lads. Is there nobody else to save in Dublin?

ELDER OSBORNE: You're looking a new man already, Michael.

THE MORMONS walk past him and take the same seats, smiling at first, although taken aback by the display on the table. BOSCO has been rooting in MICK's jacket and finds the scrap of tin foil. He turns and looks at THE MORMONS.

BOSCO: Howya lads. Com'ere, is it cool to roll? (*He suddenly darts forward*) Get up ye bastard, you're sitting on my Blu-Tack!

They jump up in alarm to look behind them and ELDER STANFORD prises it from the seat of his trousers. He hands it to BOSCO, who takes it dejectedly, trying to mould it back into the size it had been.

MICK: (*Nodding towards the door*) Bosco.

BOSCO: Oh Yeah. Nice to meet you lads. I'll see yous again. (*He is almost at the door when he cannot resist turning back to them. He produces the Blu-Tack.*) Be honest lads, what do you think? Thirty spots. Did I do well? Did I?

ELDER STANFORD: (*Confused*) Well, eh, I'm sure you did. Where did you get it?

BOSCO: That would be telling, eh. But Shay now upstairs is the man you boys should see.

ELDER STANFORD: (*Eagerly*) Shay. Oh, we will certainly give him a call. And maybe yourself?

BOSCO: (*Modestly*) Ah no, Shay is big time, get you anything you want. But I can leave you some of this when I get it.

ELDER OSBORNE: Thanks anyway, we have thumb tacks.

BOSCO: (*Stunned*) Jaysus, what do you do with those?

MICK half-lifts BOSCO towards the door as the two MORMONS stare blankly at him. MICK closes the door.

ELDER OSBORNE: Nice lad.

ELDER STANFORD: Likes sticking things.

MICK: He does.

ELDER STANFORD: Very helpful too about the poor lad upstairs. We will certainly call to comfort him.

MICK: I really won't do that. For your own safety.

ELDER STANFORD: (*Looking around*) Had you eh... a party last night?

MICK: No, no. Just myself (*He pulls on his cigarette as he tries to put conviction into his voice*) and, eh.. a few women you know. But, I won't tell you any more because you'd see you're wasting your time.

ELDER OSBORNE: No, Michael, you can be honest with us.

MICK: Ah no lads, you've been very good to call in every second night and I'd hate to disillusion you. (*He pauses, but neither MORMON replies*) Well, if you insist. They were sisters, you see... the three of them... from the West of Ireland. Very poor families there, all the children sleep in the one bed. I suppose they'd just never got out of the habit. Though of course with so much drugs and alcohol and caffeine and tobacco I don't remember much about it. It all got very confusing about who was feeling who. But then you're men of the world. You know the score yourselves.

ELDER STANFORD: (*Wide-eyed*) Hardly.

MICK: Anyway when the three of them had left... for school... and I lay here in the ashes of another night of lust, I started thinking that... well I'm not proud of the way I am, but I'm not ashamed of it either. I just guess that I'm not the saveable type. I'm sorry you boys have put in so much time and I really do appreciate it. But that's just the way it is. Don't be disheartened. There'll be others to save.

ELDER OSBORNE: Oh we're not in the least. In fact we're heartened. It is the black sheep that the good shepherd seeks. Your words only prove that God has given you to us to save. We know it will not be easy, Michael, brother...

MICK: (*In despair*) Ah now, go easy lads.

ELDER OSBORNE: We are in this together. Your misery must be great for you to wallow so deeply in filth. But all the richer will be your salvation. I want you to know our footsteps will be with yours down every inch of that long road to repentance.

MICK: (*Dejected*) Ah lads. Can't you see that I don't want repentance. All my life I just wanted to be left alone.

ELDER OSBORNE: How do you really know what you want unless you listen to your soul. When I look at you I see a lost and frightened child, but one too stubborn to cry for help. You can neither hide nor run from yourself.

ELDER STANFORD: Ambition, Michael. You have to strive for something. What do you want from life?

MICK: I'd accept a written apology. I don't know how to break this to you but I'm actually very happy in my life. Okay, maybe one day I'll get to spend all my time reading half-cracked philosophers and watching Italian football from the bed. But it's not that bad as it is.

ELDER OSBORNE: How far are you with the first book?

MICK: I haven't started the back cover yet.

ELDER OSBORNE: (*Opening his case*) Always the jokes, Michael. We'll leave you this one as well and a few magazines to pass around your friends.

MICK: (*Desperately searching for straws*) If I brought back all the library books, would that not be enough repentance for now?

ELDER OSBORNE: You only need one book, Michael. (*He leaves the pile of magazines and pamphlets down*) Spread the good word, that's what we are all here for.

MICK: (*Anxious to get them out the door*) Even if I'm not finding Our Lord with you lads, I'm certainly starting to mention his name a lot. (*He opens the door*) Now remember I may not be in much these evenings. Busy social life, especially with the Galway triplets... and their younger sister.

ELDER STANFORD: Don't worry. We'll find you, Michael.

MICK throws his eyes up to heaven as they exit. He closes the door and heads straight for the bed to climb in. There is a thunderous knocking on the door, which he ignores as he reaches for a book. The knock comes even louder and MICK rises reluctantly to opens the door an inch and then fully.

MICK: (*Disguising his alarm*) Ah, Mr Lewis, is it yourself? About the rent, I just seem to keep missing you these last weeks. Will you be around the same time on Friday?

MICK steps back to allow the landlord to enter, still in the bottom-half of his police uniform.

MR LEWIS: (*West of Ireland accent*) Ah 'tis'nt the rent at all, though I will be around on Friday. No 'tis about your visitors. They seem fierce fond of you boy, fierce fond indeed. Oh I know, Mickey, I was your age once. 'Tis an age when the oul doubt begins to creep in, especially for a young country lad like yourself cut off from your family and your native place.

MICK: I keep telling you, Mr Lewis, I'm actually from Fairview.

MR LEWIS: (*Unheeding*) Sure wasn't I in a same boat myself in this city forty years ago when I got my first posting in the guards. The oul doubt is a fierce man. 'Twould make you susceptible to alien influences, be it the drink (*looks at the table*) Or the wee-men (*looks at the bed*) or them foreign fuddy-duddy religions. No, say nothing. Sure we're all mortal. But 'tis quare company for a young lad like you to be keeping, so I'll fix it to have two friends of mine, mature people from the Legion of Mary, over here tomorrow evening to drive all that foreign nonsense out. You'll thank me for this yet, Mickey. We'll have a good laugh about it one day.

MICK: (*Horrified*) No, honestly, Mr Lewis. It's very good of you but there's no need. I'm doing everything in my power to stop them calling.

MR LEWIS: Don't try to hide it, Mickey. Sure we're all Irishmen together. 'Twould prey on me conscience if I were to see you lose the faith. They're two of the best the Legion have. Have no fear about that. We'll have you a new man in days. (*He slaps MICK heartily on the back*) God, you'll be climbing Croagh Patrick in your bare feet!

MR LEWIS exits, leaving MICK horror-struck. He closes the door, walks slowly back to the bed and climbs into it as 'Ave Maria' by Dickie Rock starts in the flat below. He pulls the bedclothes over his face as the lights go down.

Scene Four

In silhouette, moving in swift jerky motion as if in a speeded-up film, MICK leaves the bed and opens the door to MR LEWIS who, with great backslapping, mimes introducing MICK to LILY and JACK. MR LEWIS exits and LILY and JACK sit on the sofa while MICK sinks back onto the edge of the bed. Music stops and the lights come up. MICK looks petrified at the couple before him still in their coats.

LILY: You poor young fellow, caught in here like a rabbit in a trap. Sure how could you have known where to come for help?

JACK: Ah, we're always glad to help. Gets us out in the evenings too, nothing ever on that oul telly.

LILY: Lord, I envy you your youth. Oh the things we did, do you remember, Jack?

JACK: (*Looks puzzled*) I think so.

LILY: But there's so many more temptations for young people now. If you saw the state of the young ones in O'Connell St at night. Say what you like about that Boy George who used to swan around in dresses, but at least he covered his legs up!

She hits JACK with her elbow for a response.

JACK: Aye, he did that.

LILY: A sound body and a sound mind, that's what I say. But sure, t'isn't the women at all in your case Mr Lewis was telling us. 'Twould better off if you were out at a few dances instead of sitting in here brooding.

JACK: Or playing manly sports. Swinging a hurley is where you'd be safe from them Morman buckos. (*He sneaks a look at LILY*) There's great peace on the playing pitch.

LILY: It only takes one crack in your armour for every Mormon and Jehovah to come nosing in. Before an innocent young gosoon like you knows it, they have you up to your eyeballs, and you know the funny thing? (*MICK shakes his head, baffled*) You wouldn't ever know you were doing wrong. Lack of information. I blame the schools for not teaching right from wrong. Sure you could be walking through a minefield and not know it. Now, child, are you familiar with the forbidden and suspect societies, especially the ones banned under pain of sin and excommunication?

JACK: Aye, the Masons. "The faithful must beware of associations which are secret, condemned, seditious, or suspect, or which seek to evade the legitimate vigilance of the Church." Canon Law, No: 684. *(Pause)* Can you get Sky Sports on that telly, son?

LILY: "Those who give their names to the Masonic sect incur by that very fact an excommunication which is reserved, in the simple manner, to the Holy See." Canon Law, No: 2335.

JACK: *(To LILY)* No, 'tis more likely he'd be involved in something with just a simple prohibition. Like The Independent Order Of Good Templars, The Odd-Fellows or The Knights of Pythias.

LILY: Not to mention Spiritualist or Theosophical societies.

JACK: The Friends of Israel Society.

LILY & JACK: Or the Communist Party!

LILY: Which only leaves the Societies Declared Suspect or Deserving of Caution like The Young Men's Christian Association, or Rotary clubs. You were never in a Rotary club were you?

MICK: I was only ever in the Shelbourne Supporters Club.

JACK: *(Brightens up)* Wasn't Ben Hannigan a great oul player all the same. Did you ever see...?

LILY: Jack!

JACK: Oh. I think you were safe enough there son.

MICK: And I left that when I was eight. Honestly you can put your mind to rest, I've a life-long aversion to joining anything.

LILY: Still the Mormons are the sly boys. Nosing in here brainwashing and you still wet behind the ears. *(Snorts)* Polygamy how are you! Did they tell you the legend of the Golden Plates?

MICK: Well, we hadn't really got beyond foreplay.

LILY: Fabrication. More gold in a packet of Benson & Hedges. Coming in here looking for tolerance. Divil the bit they ever gave anyone themselves. If I had Brigham Young to myself for five minutes I'd grab him where the hair is short. Did they tell you about his speeches, "Every spirit that confessed Joseph Smith is no prophet is of the Antichrist." I'd give him the Antichrist. I suppose they were going to teach you to speak in tongues.

MICK: I said I'd sooner stick to the Linguaphone.

There is a knock on the door. MICK approaches it cautiously, opens it and stumbles back as SIOBHAN (in a short skirt) jumps in on him, wrapping her legs around his waist.

SIOBHAN: (*Oriental roar*) Kato! (*She slowly looks over MICK's shoulder and sees LILY and JACK transfixed by her entrance*) Good Jaysus!

MICK: (*To JACK*) Manly sports, was it?

LILY: (*Rising briskly*) Well Jack, I think we've taken up enough of this young man's time for tonight.

JACK: (*Reluctantly*) I suppose so.

LILY sweeps towards the door in JACK in tow and exits. JACK pauses.

JACK: Hello, Miss. (*He looks back into the flat*) It's great to get out in the evenings, son.

He exits and MICK slowly lowers SIOBHAN to the ground.

SIOBHAN: Sorry, Mick. I though you were alone. Who was she?

MICK: Oh, my Aunt Ellen. Up for the Christmas shopping.

SIOBHAN: In August?

MICK: A fierce cautious woman. Let's get out of here before anybody else calls.

He grabs his jacket, kisses SIOBHAN, puts his arm around her, flicks the light switch to put the bed-sit into darkness and they exit. There is brief silence, then the sound of knocking.

MR LEWIS: (*Offstage*) Mickey, they're two of the best in the Legion. I'll be into you for that back rent on Friday.

There is silence again, followed by thunderous knocking)

BOSCO: (*Offstage*) Thirty Spots, Mick. Be honest, was I robbed?

Scene Five

After a brief blackout music comes faintly from downstairs as the door opens again and, in slowly flashing light, MICK and SIOBHAN enter less drunkenly than on the first night. Initially we don't know where the light is coming from; then, as lights rise slightly, we realise that MICK has a stolen roadworks lamp under his jumper. He takes it out to look at it.

MICK: What'll I do with the shagging thing?

He places it on the table and goes over to the locker while SIOBHAN sits on the bed to remove a six-pack from a carrier bag. The lamp (along with some filled in light) lights the rest of the scene.

MICK: (*Rooting around*) Jaysus, it's just like poker, I can never get an opener. Hang on, here's one.

He rises, holding the opener and opens two bottles from her lap, raising one to his lips.

MICK: Cheers!

He sits beside her on the bed and they drink, gazing at the flashing light

SIOBHAN: Romantic, isn't it.

MICK: Yeah, like being at a rave in Cloghar Head.

SIOBHAN: When were you ever at a rave? You'd be too lazy to queue.

MICK: I'm not lazy, I'm just trying to live my life in my own way in the Independent Republic of Mickonia. It's hard enough being Monarch, Chancellor and Official Leader of the Opposition, but Minister for Defence is where my work is really cut out. Half the world is perpetually trying to annex me. Every Christmas my brother-in-laws take it as a personal insult that I don't own a car or haven't got promoted in work yet. They can't get it into their skulls that I've taken a solemn vow of apathy against their world.

SIOBHAN: That's just an excuse to be a lazy bollox.

MICK: Listen, it's lazy people who get caught up in that madness out there — licking some arse for promotion, joining a building society to save for some house, voting for the Soldiers of Density, The Warriors of Cuchulainn or The Progressive Shan Bhean Phochters. I've stepped out of that world and you won't believe how much hard work and vigilance it takes to get people to simply leave me alone.

SIOBHAN: Okay, not lazy then, but cynical.

MICK: The Cynics were the finest philosophers in the ancient world. The name comes from the Greek for dog, after old Diogenes of Sinope who founded them and was a bit of a dog himself. (*MICK briefly picks up the lamp*) He used to go around in broad daylight with one of these lit up, trying to find an honest man. Old Diogenes thought we should live without possessions or artificial complications to bind us down, scornful of sexual restraint or social institutions, as free as the dogs in the street.

SIOBHAN: That explains your sexual preferences, anyway.

MICK: (*Mock hurt*) Ah now. Diogenes is the patron saint of Mickonia.

SIOBHAN: (*Gentle teasing*) Him and Peter Pan. You're gas, you've never grown up, Mick. Was that woman really your aunt?

MICK: Sure, wouldn't I be too lazy to invent a lie? (*He puts his arm around you*) Come here to me and less of this oul chat.

SIOBHAN: I could get fond of you, you know that.

MICK: (*As serious as he can go*) Diogenes himself would make room for you in his tub.

He kisses SIOBHAN who pushes him away slightly.

SIOBHAN: That light. I feel like I'm on a building site.

MICK picks up the lantern and looks around, unable to kill its light. He opens the wardrobe, sticks it inside and closes the door, putting the stage into almost total darkness.

MICK: (*Darkly*) Okay Kato. Lesson No 157.

We hear SIOBHAN giggle as Mick jumps onto the bed. There is a pause to suggest time passing before some more light bleeds in.

SIOBHAN: (*Sleepily*) Mick? (*He mutters in his sleep.*) Wake up Mick, I have to go?

MICK: (*Sleepily*) Phone in sick for me.

SIOBHAN: Mick, wake up and put the light on. I told you I can't stay the night. Where are my clothes? Can you find my panties? It was you threw them away.

MICK: Threw them away? I thought I ate them.

He switches on the bedside lamp and begins to root around on one side of the floor nearest the audience while SIOBHAN searches the top of the bed. He finds her panties and holds them up, about to call her, before suddenly changing his mind and stuffing them down into his own underpants.

SIOBHAN: (*Pulling on her dress under the blankets*) Shag it, I'll go without them. I'll get a taxi at the rank easily enough, won't I? I suppose there's no chance of an escort?

MICK: People would think we were walking out.

SIOBHAN: If I'm murdered I'll come back and haunt you. Give us a kiss then. (*They kiss and MICK gets out of bed to see her to the door*) Friday night then, Dog. Turn up drunk and I'll kill you.

MICK: Turn up sober and I'll kill you.

He closes the door after her and turns to thoughtfully consider her panties which he removes from his underpants. He climbs back into bed and switches out the light.

Scene Six

The sound of music begins, being played by MICK. After a moment we hear knocking and the lights come up. MICK stands on the bed, holding a pitching wedge. There are a small pile of table tennis balls at his feet and a waste bin near the door with more clustered around it. He takes the cigarette from his mouth.

MICK: Mondays, Wednesdays and Fridays The Mormons. Tuesdays and Thursdays the Legion of Mary. (*He thinks*) Friday, it has to be the Church of Jesus Christ of Latter-Day Saints. (*Shouts*) Is that you lads?

ELDER OSBORNE: (*Offstage*) Nice to hear you in, Michael.

When MICK hears ELDER OSBORNE's voice he jumps from the bed, turns off the music and begins to remove all his clothes until he is only wearing the panties which SIOBHAN had lost in last scene. He takes a bag from under the bed and produces from it a bra which he fits clumsily on. He looks around, then stuffs two table tennis balls into the bra before approaching the door. He furtively blesses himself, looks heavenwards and gives a little thumbs up sign.

MICK: It's going to be a shock lads but I can't hide it any longer. You're going to have to see me as I am, a wretched, pathetic creature. (*He opens the door. THE MORMONS enter and stand in shock.*) I know. I hate to disappoint you, but I can't help myself. Now can't you see that I'm just not convertible? I mean ask yourself, am I really Mormon material?

ELDER OSBORNE: (*Shocked*) We know you were bad, Michael, but really! Elder Stanford, turn your eyes away.

ELDER STANFORD looks away, then, holding a book over his face, he takes a little furtive peep out.

MICK: (*Hopeful*) Well, I guess this is it, lads. I do appreciate you trying but...

He stops speaking as SIOBHAN suddenly walks in the open door.

SIOBHAN: Hope you don't mind me being early, Mick, I... (*She stops dead, then points.*) My knickers!

MICK: Good Jesus!

ELDER OSBORNE: Michael!

SIOBHAN turns to leave and MICK grabs her. She pulls away but he manages to hold onto her.

MICK: I can explain, honest. (*To THE MORMONS*) Lads, give me a break (*They look at him*) come on, give me a minute to myself!

Reluctantly the two men retreat towards the door as MICK leads SIOBHAN over beside the bed. She is deeply shocked, yet trying to stay cool.

SIOBHAN: I can't believe this, Mick. The only reason you took me in was probably to steal my underwear. Why bother with me? I mean I could have just sent them over in a plastic bag.

MICK: (*Embarrassed but pleading*) Come on, Siobhan, you know me better than that.

SIOBHAN: I don't. I mean I've been sleeping with a transvestite. I can't take it, Mick, I just wish you'd told me.

MICK: Give me a chance to explain, Siobhan. For the past three weeks I've had these fuckers up my arse. They're determined to convert me. I've tried everything else to get rid of them.

SIOBHAN: Have you never just tried "Go and fuck off."

MICK: Well, no, I mean I'm a man of sensibilities. I don't want to offend anybody. Now, you don't honestly think I'm a transvestite? Not somebody who follows Shelbourne?

SIOBHAN: What about the old hatchet in here the other night?

MICK: Stormtroopers from The Legion of Mary. The landlord called them in because of these boys. I'm desperate to be rid of the whole shagging lot of them.

SIOBHAN: (*Suddenly serious*) Swear to me you're telling the truth.

MICK: (*Looking down at his outfit*) Black and red — the Bohs colours? Do you have to ask?

SIOBHAN: (*Laughs*) You look ridiculous. Put some clothes on for God's sake and I'll sort these cowboys out.

He dresses while she goes over to THE MORMONS beside the door.

SIOBHAN: (*Firmly*) I'm afraid I'm going to have to ask you to leave. My friend is very upset just now and I think it would be better if you didn't call to him in future.

ELDER OSBORNE: I assure you our only thoughts are for his own welfare. Michael is in a dark night of the soul. Tell him we were not really shocked by his clothes. All these things are an attempt to escape from himself: the dressing up, the drugs, the drinking and the three little girls he had sleeping with him here one night last week.

SIOBHAN: The three little what!

ELDER STANFORD: (*Helpfully*) Three sisters. Eh, school girls I think.

He nods to ELDER OSBORNE, pleased to have been of assistance.

SIOBHAN: (*looking back*) I'll show the bastard.

She returns to MICK who is now almost fully dressed. He smiles at her, but she slaps him in the face, grabs her panties off the bed and storms out.

MICK: (*Holding his face*) What in God's name?

He looks at the two MORMONS.

ELDER STANFORD: (*Reassuringly*) Never mind Michael, you still have us.

MICK: Out!

They retreat as he approaches them menacingly, before ELDER OSBORNE rallies.

ELDER OSBORNE: Now now, Michael. This is a bad time for you but we'll stick in there. When you repent she'll come running back, anxious to join with you in the light of grace. There is a quotation here I would like to share with you.

He begins to search quickly through the pages of the large bible he carries while ELDER STANFORD parks himself happily on the sofa. There is the sound of knocking on BOSCO's door.

MICK: (*Weakly*) Piteous Christ, lads, you're destroying my life.

OLLIE: (*From the hallway*) Bosco! Are you a tad in, Bosco?

ELDER OSBORNE: Ah, here we are, John, Chapter...

There is a knock on the open door, silencing him. OLLIE and PASCAL appear with two bags and a round wooden box.

OLLIE: Howya, you seen Bos....

MICK: (*Rushing forward in desperation to fling his arms around their shoulders*) Cousin Oliver and little Pascal. Come to visit after all these years. Come in, come in.

He pulls PASCAL and OLLIE (who look completely bewildered) into the room.

PASCAL: More bucking Mushrooms?

MICK: You've come to stay, have you? It's marvellous to see yous again. (*He turns to the MORMONS*) Sorry lads. A family reunion. Fierce emotional. Eh, if you wouldn't mind, it's a bit private.

ELDER STANFORD: (*Rising*) Oh no, of course not.

ELDER OSBORNE: John, Chapter...

He looks in irritation at ELDER STANFORD who is shaking hands all around and heading for the door, then slams the book shut, and reluctantly shakes hands with OLLIE and PASCAL before he too exits. MICK closes the door behind THE MORMONS in relief and turns.

MICK: Sorry about that, lads. Drastic action called for.

OLLIE: Not at all Mickie, sure we're a tad delighted to be asked.

MICK: What?

OLLIE: I suppose you want the bed, do you? I'm a tad tired.

MICK: Wait, no...

OLLIE: Fair play to you. Really appreciate it. You'd get a tad sick of Bosco's floor inside.

He deposits the round box on the bedside table, drops his bag on the ground and with a leap planks himself full length on the bed. He stretches his boots out and snuggles down.

OLLIE: You're a tad fond of your comfort, aren't you?

MICK: I am. I was.

He watches PASCAL take off his boots, grab a packet of biscuits off the bedside table and climb into the other side of the bed, finding the bra, looking at it and then flinging it onto the floor. PASCAL and OLLIE settle down contentedly for the night. MICK stares at them, sighs and then removes a tattered old sleeping bag from the wardrobe and lays it out on the floor. He removes his shoes, trousers and top, then climbs into it.

MICK: How's Drogheda?

OLLIE: Don't ask. A town in shagging crisis, the lowest point of the low.

MICK: More factory closures?

OLLIE: Shag them. Local Government elections!

MICK: (*In sympathy*) Holy wank!

OLLIE: You can stick closures. You can stick the dole. But you know what local Government elections mean?

PASCAL: (*Splurts out*) Bucking oul Canvassers!

OLLIE: Shagging posters of the bastards!

PASCAL: (*In one breath*) Bucking handwritten notes done by bucking machine saying how bucking sad they were to have bucking missed you slipped in your bucking letterbox by bucking bastards doing the bucking hundred yard sprint down the bucking road.

MICK looks visibly unnerved by PASCAL's speech.

OLLIE: Mobile advice clinics pissing past playing Wolfe Tone records.

PASCAL: Bucking loudspeakers mounted on bucking cars.

OLLIE: No. What kills me most is people being a tad nice to you. The oul bastard of a grocer on the corner of my street. He hates me. I hate him. We're grand. Then every six months there's another election and he starts smiling at me, asking about my mother, any sign of a job, saying he'll put a word in for me.

MICK: (*Wearily*) It doesn't sound a good place to be, lads.

OLLIE: It's not, but we've a wee tad of a plan, Pascal, don't we.

PASCAL: (*In a voice filled with nervous apprehension*) Oh Jaysus, don't bucking mention that!

The lights go down for a brief period, then grow again, very faintly to suggest that dawn is approaching. A flashlight held by PASCAL is shone and we see the outline of OLLIE shoving the round box under the bed.

OLLIE: (*Whispering as he rises*) Are you right so?

PASCAL: (*Whispering back*) Call it off, Ollie. I'm bucking petrified.

OLLIE: Don't chicken out now.

They approach the sleeping figure of MICK lying in the sleeping bag near the armchair. PASCAL kneels to wake him.

PASCAL: Mickie. We're just bucking off.

MICK: (*Sleepily*) You're bucking what?

PASCAL: We're away.

MICK: (*Relieved*) Oh, great stuff.

OLLIE kneels beside him as well.

OLLIE: We're just leaving a wee tad of a parcel, Mick. We'll collect it when we're back down in a few days time.

MICK: (*Confused*) What? You're leaving what?

OLLIE: Don't bother opening it, just leave it under the bed. But look after it and don't go showing it to anybody. I wouldn't even mention this to Bosco.

MICK: (*Waking up fully*) Wait a second. What parcel? Where?

PASCAL: (*Rising*) You're a bucking mate, Mick, so you are. Bosco always said you were.

PASCAL and OLLIE creep towards the door, which they open and exit in a thin blade of light.

MICK: (*Completely awake and petrified*) Lads? Hang on a second, lads. Let's talk about this.

The door shuts. MICK scrambles up and switches on the light, blinking in the force of it. He is naked except for a pair of underpants. He looks around, then kneels by the bed to produce the box.

MICK: (*Lifting it out with trepidation*) Buck me! (*He stops*) Jaysus, I'm starting to talk like them. If this isn't stolen it will self-destruct in three minutes. (*MICK rises and carefully places the box on the bedside chest of drawers, above the secret panel. He bends his ear down to listen.*) I don't mind dying. I'm just hate being the first Irish Mormon martyr. There'd be little plastercast statues of me above doors all over Dublin. (*He raises his head*) No ticking. (*He stands back, considering*) It's too quiet for a smuggled piglet. Right!

Standing to one side, he slows cuts through the tape holding the box together, then carefully lifts the lid. A look of horror covers his face as gradually a crooked, human head is revealed. He backs away, tossing the lid of the box away from him in terror and blesses himself.

MICK: (*Mesmerised, speaking with difficulty*) The head of Oliver Plunkett! The head! (*He looks at the closed door and shouts*) Ye shagging bastards, ye shagging sacrilegious bastards! You stole the head of Saint Oliver Plunkett. (*Pause, then a shout of great indignity.*) And you left the shagging thing with me! *He sits on the edge of the bed, his hands shaking, his eyes glued to the head in disbelief.* This can't be true. God, I need a cigarette. And a drink.

He searches in the drawer for a half-finished naggin of whiskey, which he lifts it to his lips and swallows hard, before placing the bottle down on the table beside the head. His hands still shaking, he reaches for his jacket, takes out his cigarettes and, with difficulty, lights one. He inhales deeply, blows the smoke out and stares at THE HEAD. Slowly the eyes swivel to look at him.

THE HEAD: (*In a Scottish accent, as deep as the grave*) Well, don't offer them around. Can you no see I've a mouth on me too?

MICK shudders, his whole body convulsed with terror. Slowly, MICK takes the cigarette from his mouth and, as if in a dream, reaches over to place the cigarette in the mouth of THE HEAD. THE HEAD inhales deeply, then blows the smoke towards MICK's face. MICK removes the cigarette and reaching for the whiskey bottle, holds it out, offering it to THE HEAD.

THE HEAD: Naaaaaah. I've no stomach for alcohol.

MICK tilts the whiskey bottle back and swallows hard, as the lights go down.

End of Act One

ACT TWO

Scene One

The sound of music is heard from the flat beneath MICK's, then MICK's voice is heard through the darkness.

MICK: Forty-six... forty-seven...forty-eight...

Light comes up on the bed-sit. THE HEAD rants like a crazied preacher in a strong Scottish accent while MICK has his head immersed in a basin of water on the floor. MICK's appearance shows signs of not having slept all night. Throughout the second act his appearance should continue to deteriorate from shock, drink, drugs and lack of sleep. The actor playing THE HEAD (listed in the cast as a Scottish gentleman for surprise purposes) never leaves the hidden alcove built into the chest of drawers. When the trick box is placed on top of the secret panel, he slips his head into it before the lid of the box is removed. When the lid is placed back down, he withdraws his head into the chest of drawers and closes the panel before the box is lifted up again. The lighting suggests that it is early morning.

THE HEAD: Yea, weeping shall be heard from the mountain tops and eagles crisscross the sky...

MICK: (*Lifting his head with a splash of water*) Forty-nine.

MICK looks at THE HEAD and when it begins to speak again, ducks his head back into the basin.

170

THE HEAD: ...and blood run through the streets in torrents, vengeance washing over the shores, driving off the filth, the wicked and the damned...

MICK: (*Lifting head*) Fifty. (*He stares at THE HEAD which is just finishing talking.*) Good Jaysus! It's still doing it.

THE HEAD: Blasphemer! In the presence of a saint...

MICK: (*Banging on the floorboards and shouting over THE HEAD's voice*) Shut that fucking music up!

THE HEAD: ...Cursed be your seed and breed!

The music stops. MICK sits back on his heels.

MICK: Merciful hour.

THE HEAD: A plague shall cover the land. Death stalking the streets as children run to embrace him. I say to you... (*He is convulsed by a fit of coughing and his tone switches to conversational*) Will you no light up another one of those fags, for God's sake?

MICK rises to light a cigarette and place it in THE HEAD's mouth.

MICK: I didn't know saints smoked.

THE HEAD: (*The cigarette drops from his mouth as he shouts*) Didn't know! Quote me chapter and verse where it says saints shalt not smoke. I'll no argue the finer points of theology with you, ye pup ye!

MICK: I'm doing it again, talking back to it. (*MICK replaces the cigarette in THE HEAD's mouth, who puffs away contentedly as MICK rushes over to examine the piles of books on the floor, opening one and searching through it frantically*) Hallucinogenic mushrooms. Time limits for flash back. (*He looks up*) It must be them bloody farmers spraying chemicals.

THE HEAD: (*The cigarette falling from his mouth again as he resumes shouting in rhetorical tones*) And plagues of locusts strip the grass from the soil. Lo, and I say upon you, there shall be tears shed.....

There is the suddenly loud droning of an alarm clock which further unnerves MICK. He roots under the bed, takes it out, shakes it and kills the sound.

MICK: (*Hitting his own head*) Wake up! (*Stops*) Shag it, I am awake. I'm in no fit state to work. It's the stress of visitors. Take to the bed. Cold turkey. No drink, no drugs. Do something drastic. Join a monastery, join the Swords branch of the Tidy Towns competition.

He places the clock on the floor and stares sternly at THE HEAD who is observing him.

THE HEAD: (*Crossly*) Will you no sit still when I'm talking to you?

MICK: (*Desperately*) Listen, I know you don't exist, but can you not stay quiet for five minutes even.

MICK puts one finger to his lips, then opens the door cautiously.

MICK: (*Calling politely*) Bosco! (*No reply*) Shay! (*Still no reply*) Are any of yous bastards ever awake in the mornings? Anyone left in the world. (*He leans back against the wall.*) Alone in my agony.

THE HEAD: Are ye a man of faith or straw?

MICK: (*To himself*) Don't answer it. It's a warning, like those blackouts last year.

THE HEAD: Take me to the multitudes and I will speak in tongues...

MICK: Multitudes? (*He jumps forward*) I have this licked.

He approaches THE HEAD who stops speaking and regards him critically.

THE HEAD: No.

MICK: No what?

THE HEAD: No to whatever is in your mind. I can smell the sin from here.

MICK: I'm putting an end to this illusion right now.

THE HEAD: Enough talk! Prepare to go forth with my message.

MICK: You're in my mind and nowhere else. Prove yourself.

THE HEAD: Doubting Thomas! Would you put your fingers in the holes of the nails? What is this trial? I fear not your taunts!

MICK: Do you know what a telephone is?

THE HEAD: (*His voice drops to a whinge*) Of course I know what a telephone is. We've had telephones for years in Drogheda. Why is everybody always slagging Drogheda?

MICK: Well then, just one phone call to say that I'm sick. Bad cold, won't be in till Wednesday. Do that and I'll believe in you.

THE HEAD: Bad cold? There's nothing wrong with you that an honest day's work wouldn't cure. Besides I'm a saint. I can't be telling lies.

MICK: (*Catching himself on.*) What am I doing? Engaging it in conversation. (*He turns away.*) Put it back under the bed, go to work and then find those two bastards from Drogheda. Go to my doctor — wait, he just issues sick certs. Go to a real doctor.

He picks up the lid of the box and approaches THE HEAD.

THE HEAD: (*Worried*) Bring me the phone.

MICK stops with the lid suspended.

MICK: (*To himself*) Don't do this to yourself, Mick. Not even for a day's sick.

Yet the temptation is too much. He weakly drops the lid onto the bed and goes to lift THE HEAD.

THE HEAD: (*Orders*) Bring the phone to the door.

MICK: What? (*THE HEAD glares at him, demanding to be obeyed*) This is crazy. Walk out of here. (*Pulling himself together*) No, kill this illusion now so you won't have to come back to it.

MICK enters the hall where we hear him dial a number and then returns with the receiver on a long flex which he holds around the door. THE HEAD opens his mouth to speak but the words come from a concealed microphone in the receiver.

THE HEAD: (*Ultra posh, smarmy voice*) Hello. Mobile libraries. I'd like to phone in sick for Michael Flaherty... yes, a severe head cold... thank you.

MICK holds the receiver to his ear and listens.

MICK: Good Jaysus!

MICK suddenly realises that the person at the other end hasn't rung off and clamps his hand over the mouthpiece. Gingerly he replaces the receiver in the hall and returns.

THE HEAD: A marvellous machine.

MICK: (*Shocked*) He heard, he spoke to you. Jesus, you are real.

THE HEAD: I am not Jesus, but I am real and I have come with a mission in which you must play your chosen part.

MICK: (*Falling to his knees in terror*) What must I do, Master?

THE HEAD: Listen to my words. (*Voice changes*) Nights in Drogheda cathedral with only the glow of the sanctuary lamp I have dwelt on these thoughts, letting this moment draw near. Now my silence has ended. My hand drew those thugs to desecrate the holy shrine and led them to this filthy spot, my hand chose you, the most wretched of creatures, to undertake my task. And now I charge you to deliver my message. Though men may scorn, enough will hear for its purpose.

MICK: (*Cowering*) Master, give me your words. Though the world declare me mad I'll stand on Dublin's bridges and preach to whoever will listen.

THE HEAD: No, you must travel to the cathedral steps in my city of Drogheda and repeat my message there.

MICK: Give me your words.

THE HEAD: Memorise them carefully. I have shaped them in my heart and now, through you, they shall be heard.

MICK: (*Intently, grabbing a pen and paper*) Go slowly please. I took woodwork instead of shorthand.

THE HEAD: I am the eye that has dwelt in the heart of your city, the nose that smelt your decay, the ears that have heard your teeming generations. Drogheda, I am your witness, observer of life and death. (*Louder*) And I say upon you, ye have fallen from the heights of purity, drunk from the trough of greed, sinned against the rule of God, wallowed in filth like pigs in a sty. Promiscuity stalks the town, your women parade like the whores of Babylon. But it is time for repentance, time to cover the legs of your women folk. Time I came among you to guide and rule. (*He clears his throat as his voice changes from prophet to small town politician*) And so, after thirty decades of contemplation, I am putting myself forward for election to the city council and office of Lord Mayor. My people of Drogheda, on September the 13th, vote for me, Oliver Plunkett, Saint and Councillor, Independent Fianna Fail.

MICK: (*Throwing away the paper he has been writing on and springing to his feet to clamp the lid of the box quickly down over THE HEAD.*) Shag the Tidy Towns and the cold turkey — what I need is a joint!

He roots frantically under the bedclothes and produces a sliver of silver paper. He reaches under the bed and produces the Mormon book which now has no cover at all.

MICK: I don't believe it. No shagging roach paper!

There is a sudden pounding on the door.

ELDER OSBORNE: (*offstage*) Michael! Are your cousins gone yet Michael?

MICK: (*Curling himself into a ball and staring at the dope in his hands.*) Shag the roach paper. I'll chew it raw!

Music starts again downstairs, as MICK swallows the dope and the lights go down.

Scene Two

The music fades out and lights come up to suggest midday. The lid is been removed from the box so that THE HEAD is exposed but the flat is otherwise empty. The door is open and we can see MICK in the hallway holding the telephone.

MICK: (*Into the receiver*) I got the number off Bosco. Of course I opened the shagging thing, have yous gone crazy?... Yes I know Drogheda is miserable, I know there's local elections... I don't want a cut, I just want yous to shift it from my room. I don't care what you do with it... Yes ...And what did the bishop say when you phoned up?... He told you to what? Get away, where would a bishop learn a word like that? So what are you going to do... Yeah... yeah... and do what? WHAT? Now listen to me, Ollie, (*Shouts*) you're a tad bucking crazy! Ollie? Ollie?

It's obvious that OLLIE has hung up. MICK replaces the receiver, enters the flat and bolts the door. He is carrying two books and a bottle of whiskey which he places on the bed. He sits, staring at THE HEAD whose eyes suddenly swivel around to look at him.

THE HEAD: Well?

MICK: (*Jumps*) Are you at it again?

THE HEAD: Question not the mysteries of mother church. Better for ye to fall on your knees. A time will come when you will stalk the streets in rags, when the vermin and the lice shall shun you...

MICK: Bucking Cassidy and the Tad-dance Kid want to cut your ear off.

THE HEAD: (*Shocked*) Good Jaysus!

MICK: The Drogheda Fox he's calling himself now. Mother Church don't place a high value on you. They were stunningly unconcerned. So the ear in the post is next.

THE HEAD: (*Resigned*) Why not? What's another bit to me? Dig up my bones and shatter them. I'm sure you'll find a buyer for the dust. Another ear won't hurt.

MICK: (*Suddenly sympathetic*) I'm sorry.

THE HEAD: (*Surprised*) What?

MICK: I said I'm sorry. You were just landed on me.

THE HEAD: It's okay. Did you get fags?

MICK: Oh. Here.

He lights a cigarette, places it in THE HEAD's mouth and, having poured a large whiskey into a cup, begins to read one of the books beside him. THE HEAD smokes contentedly for a moment.

THE HEAD: You're great bloody company. Three centuries of silence and I get a book worm. What is it anyway?

MICK: A life of you.

THE HEAD: (*Worried*) What are you reading that for?

MICK: I'm approaching this scientifically. I know you're just a temporary apparition from stress that I'm going to exorcise with a mixture of alcohol and historical research.

THE HEAD: (*Dismissively*) I wouldn't trust them books. Written years afterwards. Everything wrong in them.

MICK: What was your mother's Christian name?

THE HEAD: You never asked your mother personal questions in my day.

MICK: Then the name of your mother's cousin who became bishop of Ardagh and Meath?

THE HEAD: (*In difficulty*) Ah... Paddy?

MICK: (*Checking the book*) A lucky guess. When did your sister Clare enter the convent in France?

THE HEAD: When... when she attained the age of puberty, my son.

MICK: (*Reading*) "Catherine, Anne, Mary." (*He snaps the book shut in triumph.*) I'm rid of you. You never had a sister Clare. Or, at least, Oliver Plunkett never had. And further more, even allowing for periods abroad, there is no reference to him having had a Scottish accent. Now all I have to do is drink my way back to sanity and your voice will be gone.

THE HEAD: (*Rants*) Oh ye doubting Thomas, ye shall...

His voice trails off as MICK waves the whiskey bottle in his face and he realises that he is having no effect.

THE HEAD: (*Quietly*) Okay then, so I'm not Oliver Plunkett.

MICK: (*Surprised*) Then who are you?

THE HEAD: (*Wearily*) George MacSpracken.

MICK: Who?

THE HEAD: George MacSpracken. Formerly of Aberdeen. Twelve years a greengrocer in Greenwich.

MICK: (*Looking at the cup*) I thought Jameson was a good whiskey.

THE HEAD: I find it hard to believe myself. I thought I put six apples in the man's pouch. Well I didn't really, but there

again I didn't know he was the King's tax collector. I mean
the profit margin on apples was never large.

MICK: (*To himself*) Apples? Cider might work.

THE HEAD: You'd probably get away with deportation now.
But people were beheaded every afternoon for less in my day.
Ah I saw Oliver from a distance in the tower. A fierce calm,
brave man. Me, I was scared shitless and I was only a simple
beheading job — first offence, nothing fancy. It was sheer
fluke it happened the same day. Never thought I looked like
Oliver, but there again, have you ever seen anybody hung,
drawn and quartered before? It took him hours to reach
Tyburn, tied face-up on a sledge. I could hear the crowds as I
waited my turn at the block, though God knows, I was only
thinking of myself. Then I was thrust into position and only
heard the executioner approach. (*Pause*) It's strange, I thought
there'd be a sharp wedge of pain and then nothingness, but
the pain was so sudden it was just like a pinprick or a rush of
air and then all dizzy lightness, the world turning upside down
as my head rolled. But no more pain or fear...like not being
awake and yet aware of everything. (*Pause*) A huge roar went
up as Oliver's sledge arrived with the soldiers and the band.
I was forgotten about, my head tossed under the wheels of a
cart... yet I was also up high, able to see everything... the
masked executioners, the crowd hushed as Oliver made his
speech, their hunger for his slaughter. They hung him first till
you'd think he was dead. But they knew their stuff and revived
him for more pain, till the hangman finally hacked his head
off and flung it into a bonfire. A priest managed to grab it and
slip it under the cart where I was. There we were, eyeball to
eyeball, me not knowing if he was dead, alive or in whatever
class of limbo I was in myself, before, Lo and behold, the
priest hauls me out in his place. Give us a cigarette, for God's
sake. I hate remembering it.

*MICK, visibly unnerved, lights one in silence and places it to
his lips. THE HEAD inhales deeply.*

MICK: (*To himself*) This has got to be true. I'm too lazy to
invent anything that complex.

THE HEAD: I was just a thief. He was a good man.

MICK: Where's his head now?

THE HEAD: Hopefully in whatever plot they buried the rest of me. He deserves a bit of peace and quiet. He'd endured enough mutilation without having priests cart his limbs off to Germany and then Downside and his head to Drogheda. It's peace the dead need to be able to pass on. You try crossing over with people gawking in at you.

MICK: But life is a crock of shite and then you die. I mean that should be it.

THE HEAD: It's no that simple or I could just vanish into oblivion.

MICK: Does it go on forever?

THE HEAD: Don't ask me. I've had no revelations or columns of angels, just the same thoughts circling round my brain.

MICK: But why did you never speak, tell somebody?

THE HEAD: It only seems like days at times and then it feels like eternity. Do you believe in God? You'd think I'd know by now. Sometimes I think it's purgatory, my punishment that could last forever. Other times I think I'm just a freak of nature. Often I sleep for decades or remember nothing and then the staring eyes are back. Always the same. Only the clothes change. The only way I know time has passed. Sometimes I lose the gift of speech, I've too terrified to utter words or if I try people just shuffle away from the glass case.

MICK: But, surely there were priests...?

THE HEAD: The clergy can be men of surprisingly little faith.

MICK: What do you want?

THE HEAD: Oblivion. Peace. This old flat of yours is grand. Quiet.

MICK: Ah now, don't be getting too comfortable. The nationwide hunt will start soon. I'm surprised they've managed to keep it quiet. They must have closed the cathedral.

THE HEAD: Not at all. Sure they've three papier mâché replicas of me. Often they stick one in when they bring me away for a hoover. How much are they asking for?

MICK: Ten thousand in used notes.

THE HEAD: (*Mocking laugh*) Big time crooks. Even so they haven't a snowball's chance. The church does not pay out.

MICK: Don't be knocking the church. They'll cough up yet. They've only another eighty thousand relics tucked away in vaults.

THE HEAD: Say what you like, but speaking as a communist, I've no time for them myself.

MICK: (*Astonished*) A what?

THE HEAD: A communist. Marxist/Leninist.

MICK: Communism wasn't even invented when you were robbing the Greenwich proletariat.

THE HEAD: I haven't waited three centuries just to talk to some lazy sod like you. Back in the 1930s we had an excellent sacristan, a self-taught man. He used to read at night, hide the books away if any priest came in. Oh, in the end I just couldn't stand the curiosity. *Give us a look* I shouted one night. Almost killed the poor fellow, but fair play. He was an atheist himself, but well read in the sciences. He took it in his stride when he got used to me. Even had a theory about my state being caused by the movement of capital. But I tell you, I got the bigger shock when he began reading to me. *Das Kapital* from cover to cover, *The Ragged Trousered Philanthropists* — a darling of a book, *The Communist Manifesto*, my God, the ideas! We sent years at it, reading and discussing. Introduced me to the Woodbine too — a far better class of cigarette than those yokes. Only thing we couldn't agree on was Trotsky. I thought he was a decent bloke, but the sacristan was fierce inflexible about the party line.

MICK: What was he doing as a sacristan?

THE HEAD: Infiltrating. Wormed his way into everything, The Legion of Mary, Vincent de Paul, tried to join the Blueshirts and the IRA. When Comrade Stalin comes he'll need the names, he'd say, He'd the biggest funeral for a layman I ever saw, and afterwards the only person who ever had an idea about me was his young son, and even then I could be wrong. But whenever the boy scouts filed past, singing *Faith of Our Fathers* I was always convinced that just when his son got to me he'd hum *Le Internationale*.

MICK: So what was all this preaching and damnation?

THE HEAD: Sure I was more terrified than you. It's bad enough coming back to life without being an imposter. Besides, whatever chance I had of getting through to you with fire and brimstone I'd have shag all with 'Workers of the World Unite'.

MICK: The voice on the telephone?

THE HEAD: A ventriloquist. Did a Novena to me at the turn of the century.

MICK: Okay then, Independent Fianna Fail?

THE HEAD: Infiltrate. Comrade Stalin will need the names.

MICK: Comrade Stalin is dead.

THE HEAD: Shag that so. Anyway I thought I pitched it a bit liberal for Independent Fianna Fail.

There is a sudden knock.

THE HEAD: (*Scared*) They've come for me already. They heard.

MICK places the lid back over the box.

MICK: (*Politely*) Who is it?

SIOBHAN: (*Offstage*) Mick, I only have a few minutes for my lunch. I need to talk to you.

MICK looks in confusion at the box, unable to make up his mind. She knocks again. He lifts it and puts it under the sofa (but where the auidence can see it), then opens the door. SIOBHAN enters, trying to stay calm, but still shaken by what happened the previous night.

SIOBHAN: (*Grins*) Hi. Michelle, is it?

MICK: Give me a break, Siobhan.

SIOBHAN: I'm only teasing. (*Pause*) What kept you so long though, opening the door? Were you...?

She pauses uncertainly.

MICK: Was I what?

SIOBHAN: (*Tentatively*) Dressing?

MICK: (*Baffled*) Dressing? (*Her meaning registers*) Ah listen, Siobhan, you got last night all wrong?

SIOBHAN: Mick, it's okay. You don't have to be bashful. I've been asking around, finding out about this. I mean it was a shock, but it's a big world. (*Pause*) Mick, I want to help you.

MICK: Oh Jaysus, not you as well! What happened to (*Sings*) "Girls just want to have fun."

SIOBHAN: Come on, Mick, it's not easy on me coming here. I just want to clear up one question. Those girls?

MICK: What girls?

SIOBHAN: The three sisters or whatever you call them. Were they... you know?

MICK: (*Baffled*) What do I know?

SIOBHAN: Well, were they girl girls or boy girls?

MICK: (*Putting his hands to his head as he collapses onto the sofa*) I don't believe this. I am hallucinating.

SIOBHAN: (*Sitting beside him*) I hear you just put on dresses and sit round calling each other Shirley and Monica. If you were simply just all being girls together I could forgive you, Mick. Naturally it wouldn't be like before, but we could still be good friends. Now what do you say?

Her foot kicks against the box and she glances down beneath the sofa before looking up with a knowing smile.

SIOBHAN: So what's in the box?

MICK: (*Springing up*) Nothing! Leave it alone.

She falls to her knees with curious excitement.

SIOBHAN: It's your dresses, isn't it. Show them to me, Mick. Come on, let's bring this out into the open.

She lifts up the box and goes to open it. MICK tries to grab it from her hands.

SIOBHAN: Let me go, Mick, you're hurting! Please, let's be honest with each other!

MICK: (*Wrestling the box free*) Just leave it, Siobhan! It's not dresses, it's...

There's a pause, while she looks at him.

SIOBHAN: What?

MICK: (*Weakly*) It's private.

SIOBHAN: I'm trying here, Mick. Listen, give me time. Maybe it might even be alright between us, it could even be fun. But you've got to be open with me, not hiding away in your little world. What's the point of my coming if you won't be honest. (*Pause*) Mick, please open the box. You've got to come out some time. (*Pause*) Open it now, Mick, or I'm going.

MICK stands, clutching the box, trying to think of something to say.

SIOBHAN: Alright then, I'm sorry for you but it's goodbye, Mick.

SIOBHAN walks to the door, pausing for a last look back at him before exiting. She closes the door over on his silent misery.

MICK: Shag it! (*He puts the box back down on the secret opening and removes the lid.*) I suppose you heard all that?

THE HEAD: Once life begins kicking you in the face it just keeps on doing it.

MICK: Well, come on then.

THE HEAD: Come on what?

MICK: Proffer me advice. Everybody else does.

THE HEAD: (*Dismissively*) I will in my bollox. You can dance through the streets in a kimono for all I care.

MICK: Convert me then. Let's get it over with.

THE HEAD: (*Puzzled*) Convert you to what?

MICK: Communism, Catholicism, whatever you're having yourself.

THE HEAD: (*Snorts*) Give over that shite.

MICK: Aren't you worried for my welfare? Don't you wish me well?

THE HEAD: (*Evil glint*) I wish you'd roll another joint.

MICK: (*Grins suddenly*) You know, I could get to like you.

MICK lights a cigarette, places it in THE HEAD's mouth and reaches for his coat. He puts it on.

MICK: I'm getting some fresh air. See if that might banish you.

THE HEAD: Out?

MICK: Social intercourse with human beings with actual bodies. Remember?

THE HEAD: (*Pliantly*) Don't leave me.

MICK: What?

THE HEAD: Don't leave me again so soon. I've been such a long time alone in that cathedral. Stay. Please.

MICK: Listen, I'm...

THE HEAD: Please.

MICK stares at him, then begins to take his coat off again.

MICK: I don't believe this. My life is destroyed and you're making me feel guilty. I never felt guilty about anything. The only people I ever felt sorry for were those Mormons and look where it got me. Guilt. I hate that. And you're doing it.

THE HEAD: (*Cajoling*) I knew you'd be a good lad, kind to an old person.

MICK: Shut up. (*Looks around*) What'll we do for the afternoon?

THE HEAD: (*With a sly grin*) Poker.

MICK: You play poker?

THE HEAD: Not very well. Just straight. (*Pause after each name*) And five card stud. And seven card. And Southern Cross. And Klondiky. And blind baseball.

MICK: Get away.

THE HEAD: A reformed gambler in the 1940s had a great devotion to me. Loan an old man five pounds, will you? My mind is befuddled but sure you can keep winning it back.

MICK: Okay. Okay. Straight poker, jacks to open.

MICK reaches in his pockets to produce a crumpled fiver which he places down beside THE HEAD. He pours himself another whiskey and takes up a deck of cards from the bedside locker.

THE HEAD: You deal. And roll us a blast of the good stuff.

MICK looks round, then props a toast rack sideways in front of THE HEAD and places five cards on it, facing THE HEAD.

THE HEAD: I'll open for a pound. Two cards please. The last two (*MICK goes to remove them*) No looking to see what they are.

MICK: (*Giving him new cards*) I don't cheat. The sooner those spacers return you the better.

THE HEAD: Sure the whole thing happened before. I'll raise you fifty quid.

MICK: You only have a fiver. When?

THE HEAD: A mad Black-and-Tan made off with me back in 1921. The bet is fifty pounds, you'll see my money when you see my hand.

MICK: I thought all Black-and-Tan's were mad. (*He shows his cards*) Two pair.

THE HEAD: This fellow was by the time I'd finished with him. A house of Jacks.

MICK: On your first hand? Very dodgy George. Had he any joy?

THE HEAD: Not a tosser... he left me back at dead of night. Where's me fifty quid?

MICK: (*Dealing again*) I don't have it. (*Looks around*) Take the television.

THE HEAD: You better not only get RTÉ. (*Pause*) Mick?

MICK: What?

THE HEAD: Don't send me back.

MICK: What am I suppose to do with you?

THE HEAD: Anything. Just don't send me back to those gaping eyes. Bury me in a hole, put me in the fire. It would just be a moment's pain and then maybe oblivion. Okay, I might still exist as a speck of ash, but I'll take that risk. Just don't send me back.

MICK: Listen, I had a grand life before you, the Mormons, the Legion of Mary and half of Drogheda descended on me. As soon as possible I'm getting you off my hands and from there on it's your problem, George. Now can you open?

THE HEAD: Please, Mick.

MICK: I'm piling the furniture in front of that door, taking to the bed with a packet of Alpen, a twenty spot of dope and the world can go and shite. No offence, Comrade. Now yes or no? How many cards?

THE HEAD: I'll open, one card. Think about it, Mick. All those years of faces clouding the glass, hoping for cures.

MICK: (*Uncomfortable*) Just play the cards, George. Stop putting your life on my shoulders.

THE HEAD: Petrified children backing away... Raise you fifteen quid.

MICK: The blankets are worth twenty. I'll see you for five.

THE HEAD: What am I suppose to do with blankets?

MICK: What are you going with a television when you're back in your glass case? (*Shows his cards*) Three nines.

THE HEAD: Don't mention that kip. A house, fives and sevens.

MICK: Ye bollox. How do you do it?

THE HEAD: How could I cheat? I don't even have hands.

MICK: You're still going back. Do you hear?

His voice drops to a whisper as footsteps approach the door. There is a knock and SHAY's voice is heard.

SHAY: (*offstage*) No post at all this evening, Mick. What more proof do you want? Don't forget the poker session tonight.

MICK and THE HEAD stare furtively at each other, until the footsteps retreat.

MICK: Here, shag this, take the whole flat. I need a kip before these boys arrive and (*He sniffs under his armpit*) a shower.

THE HEAD: We never needed showers in my day...

MICK: (*Lifting up the lid of the box*) I hate to break it to you, George, but you do now!

In the flat below 'The Cards of the Gambler' begins to play as MICK lowers the lid and the stage plunges into darkness.

Scene Three

There is the noise of running water, then of knocking, growing louder. MICK emerges from the shower in silhouette in rapid jerky movements like a speeded up film. He answers the door and BOSCO and SHAY enter at the same speed, carrying six-packs as they settle down to open the bottles and play cards. The record dies as the lights come back up, with the fire obviously lit in the fire-place. MICK is just wearing jeans, has a towel around his neck and his hair looks wet. They are playing cards on the coffee table. SHAY sits on the sofa, BOSCO on a small stool and MICK in the bed. The box has been moved to where we can see it under the bed. They are arguing. The six-packs around them are in active use.

SHAY: We almost had to break the door down. You must have been having a good time in here with The Sacred Heart Messenger.

MICK: Don't be slagging the Sacred Heart Messenger. My mother attracted the da through it.

BOSCO: What? Did she advertise?

MICK: No, she wet the cover and rubbed the red ink on her face as rouge. I told you, Shay, you caught me in the shower.

SHAY: I thought you'd finally cracked up. Too many black-and-white movies in the afternoon. Every time the sun shines you close the curtains, put on the electric fire and stick your head in a book or watch Bilko or Bonanza. You'll go blind.

MICK: My afternoons are always quiet. Can anybody open?

All mutter "No" and throw their cards back in.

MICK: Stoke the pot. Kings or better.

BOSCO: You'd be better off buying a video, watch something good like *ET*.

SHAY: (*Snorts*) That Cavan bastard. Ah come on, Mick. Just once play something else.

MICK: House rules. Poker variations only. Dealers choice.

BOSCO: How could ET be a Cavanman?

SHAY: Sure, doesn't he look like one. Right, deal them so.

MICK: Don't mention Cavanmen. Did I ever tell you about the time I stopped for a pint in Bailieborough?

SHAY: You did not. Now just deal, will you, I'd like to actually finish a hand.

MICK: (*Dealing*) I ordered a pint of Guinness in a pub there and I'm drinking away, minding me own business when this local walks in and says to the barman, (*Cavan accent*) "giz a pint of rat, Joe."

SHAY: Me granny!

MICK: So the barman takes this dead rat from the fridge, stuffs it in a pint glass, fills it with water and hands to him. Your man throws it back straight, slaps the glass down, and orders "Another pint of rat, Joe."

BOSCO: Beats shagging Murphy's anyway.

MICK: So he says to me, "What's the Guinness like." "Grand," I said. "How's the rat?" "Best pint of rat in the county," he says, "Men come from miles to have it." So I thought, shag this, I'll try it and I say to the barman, "Throw us on a pint of rat." Well he takes this big one out, but I'm starting to get cautious now, so I say "I'll just have a glass to start." Anyway the barman can't fit the rat into the small glass so he bites its head off, shoves the rest of the body in and fills it up with water. "Well you can shag off", I said to him, "I'm not drinking that..."

BOSCO: Quite right too.

MICK: "...there's no bleeding head on it!"

SHAY laughs and looks down at his hand.

SHAY: Can anybody open? Change the game, Mick. Klondiky, Seven Card Stud, Southern Cross, they're all poker variations. Why do you always deal straight?

MICK: I like it.

SHAY: But nobody can ever shagging open.

MICK: That's why I like it. Aces high. Stoke the pot. (*They throw more money in.*) What the hell is that, Bosco?

BOSCO: Butter vouchers. They're worth 55p each.

SHAY: (*Indignant*) There's no rule in poker says we have to accept butter vouchers.

BOSCO: What's wrong with them? Do you not eat butter? Do you not have toast in the morning?

MICK shuffles and deals again.

SHAY: Of course I've shagging toast. I eat Weetabix, then I have shagging toast, but I'm still not accepting butter vouchers in the pot. Now are we playing cards or talking?

BOSCO: You're lucky to able to afford Weetabix. Try that on the dole. One pound, ninety-seven, down in the twenty-four hour shop.

MICK: (*Interrupting*) I've had a trying day, lads. I'd like a bit of relaxation. Can anybody open?

SHAY: That's bleeding robbery. They're only one pound, thirty-five in The Shopping Basket.

MICK: Ace high lads. Openers?

BOSCO: Well Super Crazy Prices is the best place. I know you have to walk across town to get there, but one pound, nineteen. I mean is that value or is that value?

SHAY: Robbing bastards in the Twenty-Four Hour. What do you think of the new Alpen?

MICK: (*Shouts*) Can you's open?

They look down.

SHAY & BOSCO: No.

MICK: Stoke the pot, no butter vouchers. Kings high. What are you putting in now, Bosco?

BOSCO has thrown a packet onto the table.

SHAY: Ohhhh — Johnnies. The hard man, Bosco.

MICK: You roll them down over your dick, Bosco. You don't use them in poker.

BOSCO: I'm broke. They worth a pound anyway.

MICK: What are you doing with Johnnies anyway? Is the teddy bear afraid of getting Aids.

BOSCO: No, for the dope.

SHAY: What?

BOSCO: So I could stick the dope inside one and swallow it if the cops arrived.

MICK: Good Jaysus. Alright, going cheap for a pound. Will somebody roll a number?

SHAY: You don't swallow Blu-Tack, Bosco, you just stick it under your tongue.

All laugh except BOSCO.

BOSCO: Bitch never showed up! Took me money and all.

SHAY: All you had to do was knock. I've the best of stuff. (*He looks down*) Shite, there's a fly in my drink.

SHAY roots around the lip of his bottle with his finger as everyone throws money into the pot. MICK deals again as SHAY holds his finger up, examining the fly on it. He squeezes his finger.

SHAY: (*To the fly*) Spit it back out, you thieving bastard!

SHAY flicks the fly away and reaches into his jacket to take out a piece of hash in silver foil.

SHAY: Five Card Stud then. Blind baseball. Why do you keep doing this to us, Mick?

BOSCO: It's awful that, getting a pint with no head.

MICK: Just open, Bosco, right.

BOSCO: (*Glancing at his cards*) I can't. Anyway those lads who were here in the dark suits thought that I got a good deal for the size of it.

SHAY: You mean the headbangers from Drogheda who've been camped on your floor for the past month?

BOSCO: No. The two fellows who are in here with Mick every second afternoon. They look like they've a few bob on them. You should ask them to hang on for a poker session some night, Mick.

SHAY: I don't know them.

MICK: (*Embarrassed*) They're nobody. Shut bleeding up, Bosco.

BOSCO: You must know the lads in the suits and dark glasses. Nice guys. They were asking me where I got the thirty spot and I think they said they were planning to give you a call.

SHAY: (*His paranoia returning*) What suits and glasses?

MICK: I'll murder you, Bosco.

SHAY: You shut up, Mick. Keep talking, Bosco. Who are these boys?

BOSCO: Ah, they're just mates of Mick who often call in to him for a chat. Posh looking lads with short hair in dark suits.

SHAY: It's the Branch. (*Stands up*) The bleeding Special Branch. You're a grass aren't you? My God, I'm playing cards with you and you're passing on every scrap of information. And I used to supply you cheap too!

MICK: Shay, will you sit down. It's not the Branch. They're just friends, they're Mor...

SHAY: You're dead, do you hear me! Don't try and tell me anybody who owned a suit would be a friend of yours, let alone (*pointing to BOSCO*) talk to that spare.

BOSCO: I had a suit once!

SHAY: And the judge called you the accused. (*To MICK*) I'm getting my gear and those plants out of here, but I've got friends, right, and the boys in the trench coats will come looking for you one of these nights. (*He darts forward to grab MICK's kneecap*) Black-and-Decker, Black-and-Decker.

He exits leaving MICK speechlessly looking at BOSCO. There is a moment's silence before BOSCO suddenly begins to laugh.

BOSCO: There's no bleeding head on it! I get it now. That's your best one yet. (*Puzzled*) Jaysus, Shay got fierce narkey.

MICK: (*Rising*) Get out! Just leave me alone.

BOSCO backs away towards the door with MICK advancing on him. But just as he reaches it there's a knock and BOSCO opens it.

BOSCO: Ah howya, lads. We were just talking about you.

BOSCO exits and THE MORMONS enter.

ELDER OSBORNE: That's the stuff, Michael. Spreading the word among your friends!

MICK: Just piss off, right, leave me alone.

ELDER OSBORNE: (*Tuts*) Language, Michael, and cards and drink. Still trying to fight yourself. Don't give up now when we were making such good progress. (*Firmly*) To business. I think we had dealt with most of your historical problems about polygamy the evening when you had to go off to your embalming classes but I detected a few reservations about the twelve apostles whom Christ chose from among the Nephites after he came from Palestine to America. (*They both take their seats on the sofa*) Well, to continue our discussion I would like to read to you from...

SHAY appears around the door with a carrier bag in one hand and a puny hash plant in the other.

SHAY: (*Shouts*) Dead, do you hear me, dead.

He sees THE MORMONS and stops.

ELDER STANFORD: (*Rising eagerly to greet him*) But born again in the immersion of Baptism.

SHAY: Good Jaysus, even the police have found God.

He exits quickly.

ELDER OSBORNE: (*Scowling at ELDER STANFORD as he reaches into his briefcase for a book*) The Nephites. When Christ reached America after his resurrection once again he had to choose...

MICK: No, I said out! You're like vultures around me neck. Before I met yous I had friends, I had a woman, I...

ELDER STANFORD: Had you found your way to God?

MICK: No! And I'll find it by my shagging self. You're all the same, Mormons, Jehovahs, Catholics, Moonies, circling round, looking for weaknesses. That's what you want, people too terrified to make decisions, people so stunned that anybody gives a fuck about them that they'd jump into the Liffey if you asked.

ELDER OSBORNE: Elder Stanford and I...

MICK: You're not elders, you're bleeding nippers. I'm five years elder than the pair of yous. Listen, I've seen your converts, middle-aged men in suits having orgies of ice cream, following the rules for an APEX ticket to Heaven. Don't tell me about sin. I'll tell you, I've lied and cheated, I'd ride a nun's arse through a church railing, but whatever the fuck is out there when I keel off this planet I'll face It or Him or Her or Nothingness in my own way on my own.

MR LEWIS: (*Offstage*): There's two weeks rent due. Shamus! And what about that ESB bill? Come back here, you owe me money.

SHAY: (*Offstage*) Let me go! This place is crawling with shagging cops!

MR LEWIS: (*Offstage*) And I'm one of them.

SHAY storms into the room, pursued by MR LEWIS. SHAY ignores everyone, walks straight across the bed and stands by the window furtively trying to eat the leaves of his dope plant. MR LEWIS stands confronting THE MORMONS.

ELDER STANFORD: Good evening sir.

MR LEWIS: I've warned you before, Mickey. Have you no sense, boy?

MICK: Do you mind if I fix you up next week?

BOSCO appears eagerly at the door.

BOSCO: What this? Another poker session already?

He is pushed into the room by LILY and JACK who appear suddenly in the door.

LILY: (*Advancing*) There they are, sneaking in! I had Jack at the end of the road watching out for yous.

JACK: (*Closing the door behind him*) Aye. It beats sitting in these evenings.

LILY: Well, you can take your hands off him, because he's a one-hundred per cent good Catholic boy and he'll never be anything else. (*She grabs hold of MICK's arm.*) Do you hear?

ELDER OSBORNE: Michael is an intelligent boy. Let him make his own mind up. We'll have no kidnapping here. (*He grabs MICK's other arm*) Don't worry, Michael, we're here to protect you.

MR LEWIS: And I'll have the last four weeks' rent if you don't mind.

As he makes a dive for MICK's pocket there is a loud knock on the door which freezes everyone.

MICK: (*Puzzled*) I don't know anybody else.

LILY and ELDER OSBORNE release MICK and he opens the door to A STRANGER in a long trenchcoat standing in the hallway. The angle of the door means that he cannot see the crowd inside.

STRANGER: (*Northern Ireland accent*) Are you Michael? (*MICK nods. THE STRANGER continues darkly*) A "friend" asked me to pay you a call.

MICK: (*Backing away scared and calling*) Shay, I like my kneecaps as they are.

STRANGER: I work with Siobhan in the tax office.

MICK: (*With intense relief*) You're from the... tax office...

STRANGER: Why shouldn't I be? We're not *all* scruffy haired beatniks in the tax office, you know.

MICK: Listen, this is just a bad time.

STRANGER: I know all about it, you poor lad. Siobhan came to me for advice, you see, the girls often do. I mean they're only human, it's hard for them to understand some things. She asked me to apologise to you. It was the shock she said, but, and these are her words, you are what you are and she knows you are a good person at heart. She gave me these for you. Herself and all her friends spent the afternoon choosing them in Penneys. (*He hands MICK a parcel*) I suggested the undies with the pink lace, I hope you like those especially.

MICK: Ah hang on now, just who the hell are you?

STRANGER: Sean, but my friends call me Sharon, the topless waitress! (*He drops his overcoat to reveal a French maid's outfit which leaves most of his chest exposed.*) And you can too! Sure we're all girls together!

MICK: Holy wank!

MICK steps back in shock and THE STRANGER enters, seeing the group gathered on the far side of the room.

STRANGER: (*Shocked*) Auntie Lily!

LILY: (*Hysterical*) My little Sean! A Jehovah Witness!

JACK: (*Consoling*) A topless waitress love, a topless waitress.

LILY: Oh thanks be to God!

STRANGER: I can't hide it any longer, Aunt Lily. I'm a TV.

MICK: At least you're not a PD.

JACK: Hello, Sean.

STRANGER: Hello, Uncle Jack.

JACK: Will this hobby last longer than the wine making?

STRANGER: Don't be cruel now, Uncle Jack.

LILY: A waitress. I need a cup of tea. None of my family were ever in service before. (*She sits down*) Tell me, Sean, you haven't lost the faith?

STRANGER: Of course not, Aunt Lily. Sure where else would you get the fashions. Here, I'll be mother.

THE STRANGER begins to fill the kettle.

ELDER STANFORD: Just hot water for me please.

ELDER OSBORNE: (*Sitting down to take LILY's hand*) You poor woman. The shame of it.

LILY: You see them come into the world, you raise them up...

ELDER OSBORNE: Oh I know... the pain of it too.

JACK: (*Going over to THE STRANGER*) How's the mother keeping, Sean?

STRANGER: The very best, Uncle Jack.

ELDER STANFORD seems transfixed by THE STRANGER and follows his every move, gazing intently at him.

LILY: (*To ELDER OSBORNE*) He was always such a good boy. (*She looks over at THE STRANGER*) Could you not cover yourself up, Sean, get a nice modest dress. There are some lovely ones in Clery's.

STRANGER: (*Coming over to her*) I know the very ones you mean, Aunt Lily.

LILY: Good material. To keep you warm in winter.

ELDER OSBORNE: It's very important that in your climate.

LILY: Oh I imagine it can be very cold standing on doorsteps.

ELDER OSBORNE: Well, of course, we only use the very best material.

He lets JACK and THE STRANGER feel the lining on his jacket

JACK: Powerful material. I remember during the emergency when you couldn't get cloth for love or money...

MICK has been watching all this happen without anyone paying him the slightest attention. Now he shouts suddenly.

MICK: Right! Every one of yous, out of my flat now!

There is a stunned silence.

LILY: Just a moment, young man. I didn't come here to be insulted.

MICK: I don't give a shite why you came here...

ELDER OSBORNE: Michael! That's no way...

JACK: (*Interrupting*) Listen here, son, you can't just walk in here and start using language to my wife.

MICK: I live here. This is my home. It's you that's after walking in.

LILY: But only for your own good.

ELDER OSBORNE: We had you down as a chronic case, Michael, but I never knew you needed our help this bad.

MICK: God, save me from those who want to do me good. You even have that sawn-off gauleiter at it now. (*He points to MR LEWIS*) We had a fine relationship before, (*MR LEWIS smiles in agreement*) he simply exploited me.

MR LEWIS: (*Frowns*) What do you mean?

MICK: Now even he wants to do me good. If you want to do me good then leave me alone. Can't you see that all I want is to be left to myself...to eat scuttery kebabs, white bread and scabby packets of soup with E's in them, to read books in Latin and watch Open University programmes at five in the morning about frogs fucking and the homosexual tendencies of the ten-spined stickleback. To do ...I don't know... anything except be a part of whatever the hell you're all into. (*Pause*) Listen, I'm going to die, I've X number of years left. I'd like to get on with them in my own way and my own time, so it's very nice of yous, but it's none of your business. Now good night and thanks for calling.

There is a silence as everybody stares at him.

MR LEWIS: (*Drawing himself up to his full height*) I'll not stay here to be insulted. You owe me three weeks rent, Bosco Ignatius.

BOSCO heads for the door with MR LEWIS in pursuit and SHAY making a break for it behind them.

JACK: God, you've a fine voice, son. You wouldn't think of coming down to the local Fianna Fail cumann.

STRANGER: (*To LILY*) It's dear for dresses Clery's though.

LILY: (*To ELDER OSBORNE*) You despair of helping some people. Well, I'll not have Irish hospitality abused. The Legion House is only around the corner if anybody would like a good strong cup of tea.

STRANGER: I'd love a cup, Aunt Lily.

ELDER STANFORD is still staring at THE STRANGER. Now he plucks up courage, touches THE STRANGER's bare arm and speaks in a voice which has dropped its textbook authority and is filled with childish wonder.

ELDER STANFORD: What does it taste like... as it slides down your throat?

The room is transfixed by the question.

STRANGER: What?

ELDER OSBORNE: Tea.

MICK: (*Roars*) Out!! Everyone! Go and save somebody else.

They all rise and troop, bristling with wounded expressions, past MICK who stands by the door. JACK is the last to leave. He pauses beside MICK, about to start a friendly chat.

JACK: It's been great getting out in the evenings. Sure, I could call round myself some time for an oul chat...

MICK shoves him out the door and slams it. He draws the two bolts shut and leans against the door frame. There is silence for a moment, before a loud knock startles him. He jumps, holding the back of his head as if it had received a blow.

OLLIE: Hey, you in there, we're a tad in a hurry. We've come for the yoke.

MICK: What?

OLLIE: Open up, Mick. All we need is the ear. We'll leave you the rest if you want.

MICK stares at the box under the bed, clearly trying to make his mind up about something. He looks back at the door, rubbing his hands nervously. Then he rushes over to grab the box and hurls it into the heart of the fire. A large spurt of flame shoots up, its reflection lighting the stage, while PASCAL and OLLIE pound on the door. MICK stares at the fire, then rises and draws the bolts back. He opens the door.

OLLIE: (*Entering*) Jaysus, what kept you?

MICK: I had something to do.

OLLIE: They stuck another head in its place. Would you believe it? But the severed ear is bound to work. They'll not outsmart the Drogheda fox. We'll give you a wee tad of a cut, Mick. We were always going to. Where is it?

MICK points to the fire. OLLIE and PASCAL rush towards it.

PASCAL: There's the bucking box. Buck it. (*He tries to reach it with his hands, but is unable to*) A poker? Have you a bucking poker.

OLLIE: (*Grabbing MICK*) You, you spacer, you animal. Have you a poker?

MICK: No.

OLLIE: (*Throwing MICK violently onto the bed*) Murderer. You bad bastard. We were always going to put it back, no matter what. They could have glued the ear back on. Have you not got a tad of respect for anything? Have you no respect for culture, for the past, no respect for your heritage? If it's one thing I hate it's you city slickers with your pluralist society, kinky sex and rock and roll. Well, I'm proud to be an Okie from Muskogee. That's my culture you're burning.

PASCAL: (*Kneeling beside the fire place*) The head of Oliver Plunkett burning. (*He crosses himself*) Saint Oliver, we didn't mean any bucking harm. We were only... and it was all Ollie's idea.. (*He thinks*) Drogheda. Bucking Drogheda without the bucking head. You take away the head and what have you left. Buck all. Oh, nobody will know, but I will. When I walk down the town and look into the Cathedral I'll know it's gone, gone forever. (*He turns to OLLIE who is attempting to strangle MICK on the bed*) I can't bucking watch the box burst open. Jesus, it's disintegrating. Oh the bucking box is bucking bucked... buck it!

PASCAL runs from the room. OLLIE sees him go, takes one terrified look at the fireplace and then races after him. MICK picks himself off the bed with difficulty and goes over to close the door. He draws the bolts again and limps towards the fireplace, hunching down to stare reflectively into the flames. There is silence.

THE HEAD: (*Speaking from the shower*) Fair play to you, son. I knew you wouldn't let me down. (*Pause*) But if you don't dry me off soon I'll get me death of cold in this shower.

MICK rises and goes to the shower unit. He comes out with his back to the audience, carrying something and places it down on the table. When he steps back THE HEAD is there, very wet looking and blindfolded.

THE HEAD: Your modesty is touching, Mick, but I have seen a dick before.

MICK: I'm particular about who I share my shower with.

He takes the blindfold off and starts to dry THE HEAD.

MICK: You're on probation, do you hear me? You shower more than once every three centuries for a start.

THE HEAD: I survived long enough...

MICK: And cheat again at cards and you're going back to that cathedral in a basket.

THE HEAD: Stop accusing me of cheating, Mick. I have feelings too. Besides if you don't, I won't show you how it's done.

MICK: Do you think I'll ever be sane again? I mean I must be crazy, but I'm starting to prefer your company, George.

THE HEAD: We're two of a kind, Mick. The little men of history, unimportant, overlooked, just getting on with living as best we can. You've only been hounded for three weeks. I've been hounded for three centuries. But it's a great rest we'll have now, and great sleeping in the long nights after Samhain. Just the pair of us, Mick. Put a bit more wood on that fire will you.

MICK tosses some bits of an auctioneers sign on the fire and pulls the wardrobe over to block the door.

MICK: Will I ever get her back, do you think?

THE HEAD: Advice, Mick? You want advice?

MICK: Forget I spoke. (*He looks at his watch.*) Twenty past twelve already. (*He thinks*) Open University.

He switches on the television and settles back on the bed, lighting up two cigarettes, one of which he gives to THE HEAD.

MICK: Did you ever see anybody roll a seven-skin joint before?

THE HEAD says "No" as best he can with a cigarette in his mouth.

MICK: Watch closely so.

MICK takes out a packet of skins and sets to work.

TELEVISION PRESENTER: The next programme is in the second-year course on biology and will deal with the reproductive system of the African fire fly.

THE HEAD: (*Looking at the screen and dropping his cigarette in shock*) Get up, ye animal ye! Oh this fellow's a randy wee divil.

MICK: I'll bet you two-to-one he'll drop the hand on that fly on the second leaf.

THE HEAD: Not at all. The one waving her arse in the air crawling down the stem. Twenty pounds says he'll park his shoes under her bed.

They both watch with bated breath.

MICK & THE HEAD: (*Wide-eyed*) Get away!

Lights fade.

THE END